40 UNDER 40

A GUIDE TO NEW
YOUNG TALENT WITH SEDUCTIVE IDEAS
FOR LIVING TODAY

Vitae Publishing, Inc.

Grand Rapids, MI

TO ALL MY FRIENDS IN THE HEARTLAND
WHO HAVE BROADENED MY HORIZONS.
– Beverly Russell

Published in the United States
by Vitae Publishing, Inc.
50 Monroe NW
Suite 400
Grand Rapids, MI 49503
800-284-8232

Library of Congress
Cataloging-in-Publication Data

Russell, Beverly.
40 UNDER 40 : a guide to new young talent with seductive ideas for living today /
by Beverly Russell
p. cm.
Includes index
ISBN 1-883065-10-0
1. Architecture, Modern – 20th century – United States.
2. Architecture – United States.
3. Interior decoration – United States – History – 20th century.
I. Title. NA712.R85 1995
720' .92'273 – dc20 - - 95-22826 CIP

VITAE PUBLISHING, INC.
CHAIRMAN - JOHN C. AVES
PRESIDENT - JAMES C. MARKLE
VICE PRESIDENT - GREGORY J. DEKKER

40 UNDER 40
Editor - Beverly Russell
Designer - James C. Markle
Communication Manager - Christine H. Hoek
Production Operations Manager - Douglas Koster
Production Artist - Nancy J. Allen

Printed in Singapore
Typeset in USA by Vitae Publishing, Inc.

Cover: Miami house by Jorge Hernandez
Photographer: Steven Brooke

Title Page: Florida house by Brian Healy
Photographer: Kimberly Holcombe

CONTENTS

FORTY UNDER FORTY: A MEMOIR

In 1966, I had just turned twenty-seven and was back in New York after leaving Yale when Philip Johnson asked me to run the programs at the Architectural League. Looking over its history, I came upon an exhibition the League had sponsored in 1941, naming forty promising architects under forty years of age. That idea seemed worth revisiting; needless to say, as a very young architect it very much fit in my own experience and interests. As a recent editor of *Perspecta, the Yale Architectural Journal*, I was familiar with the contents of the early issues, especially the first one, published in 1952, which contained a wonderful essay written about youth and age in architecture by Henry-Russell Hitchcock, the architectural historian. It was an account of the careers of the modernist architects Frank Lloyd Wright, Mies van der Rohe, and Le Corbusier as they related to their fortieth birthdays. In each case, Hitchcock pointed out that when they were forty they were well known, about to break through to maturity, but hadn't quite got there. So fascinated was I with this issue, I asked Adolf Placzek, the Avery Librarian and historian, to test the validity of the argument further, looking at careers of architects outside the modern movement. His article was titled "Youth and Age in Architecture." On the basis of this research, I was convinced, and so remain: forty is a critical age, marking the entrance to productive midlife in a professional career that usually begins in one's early thirties and winds down in one's late sixties – or later.

The French talk of a "crise à quarante ans." But being forty isn't only about crisis. Very many of us have a feeling when we reach forty that we know where our lives are going. But, because architects move more slowly in their careers than painters, musicians, or other creative artists, not to mention other professionals like doctors or lawyers, and because architecture is based on getting other people to trust you with an awful lot of money, it is hard to make a mark and to get anything built before you are forty. All the more reason to celebrate those who get something done.

The idea of a show about young architects appealed to me in another way. In 1966, it seemed to me that there was a lot of new talent around. I believed that architecture was at a turning point – my contacts with Aldo Giurgola, Charles Moore, and especially Robert Venturi, all then about forty years old, convinced me that a new phase was at hand. Of course, putting together a show about young architects gave me a chance to showcase not only the almost established but also those who promised to be established, like Charles Gwathmey. With characteristic immodesty, I included a work of my own in the show. (To Philip Johnson, I owe a special debt for this. He said that if I didn't believe in myself, who else would. He said it was perfectly right for me to put my first house in the show and very kindly wrote the text panel.) The 1966 selection had yet another aspect which I look back on with particular fondness. Although Johnson and Robert Cutler and Robert Jacobs were a committee I reported to, I alone made the choices for the show. And I think my pickings were pretty good. The show really helped to identify people as a group united not by ideology but by achievement and promise.

Most under-forty architects who were named in 1966 went on to become important practitioners. One rule in making the selection I had established, after a conversation with Philip Johnson, was that the architects chosen had to be doing work on their own. Of course, young architects often have important roles in large architectural firms long before they rise to partnerships, and there is everything to celebrate about that. But if you are going to establish your own identity on your own terms, without the support system of an existing office, then you must do it by the time you are forty. If you don't do it before you are forty, history seems to suggest you may never — but of course there are wonderful exceptions like Louis Kahn, who was in his fifties before he began to do notable independent work.

In 1966, this country was at the height of a long-lasting building boom that promised to go on forever. Single-family houses were being commissioned in a great number of places and young architects were being given a chance to experiment.

The 40 UNDER 40 show of 1966 enjoyed a certain success and seemed a kind of bellwether. In 1976, I was asked by Toshio Nakamura, editor of *Architecture & Urbanism,* to make another survey along the same lines. By this time, the economy had taken a complete nosedive, the nation was in the middle of the oil crisis, and the endless summer vacation of the mid-1960s seemed over. But the social seriousness of the moment was giving rise to really good work. Under the banner of post-modernism, the values of modernism were under siege but already a reaction of sorts was under way. Robert Venturi published his book *Complexity and Contradiction in Architecture* in 1966, which decried the self-imposed limitations of 1920s modernism. But his *Learning from Las Vegas* (1969), written with Denise Scott Brown and Steven Izenour, took the argument about cultural inclusiveness much further — some would still say too far — re-establishing architecture as an art of communication and thereby putting it in oppo-

sition to those who chose to proclaim it a pure art.

With the 1986 selection of 40 UNDER 40 it seemed time for a change of cast. The selection was made by a young architect, Andrew MacNair, with Philip Johnson and me looking over his shoulders. The eighties were at their zenith: a madly energetic time of tremendous affluence and tons of construction. But the prosperity left many people so-to-speak out of the loop and not a little embittered. Many young architects were turned off by what they saw being built, but they did not seem to have an alternative except to pursue their goals outside traditional practice. In a reaction against so much bad work, some of the best young brains began to eschew architecture as a building art and to take it up as a studio art or a literary art. This was very interesting but I think not really to the point. I was disappointed and still am. A lost generation?.

Not so the current 1996 group, which is very impressive because of its commitment to building. One thing seems very clear from the work of today's young. Fine architecture is going to flourish in the next millennium. Today's forty are too busy learning their craft to waste time predicting the end of their profession. The simple core idea commands their attention: to build responsibly and beautifully. Today seems not a time of iconoclasm but one of rediscovery. The tradition of modernism is better understood today than ever before. The past is more than ever with us — not so much revived as reinvented. What we have, dare I say, is a post–modern modernism. And it's great. I exult in the new forty.

Robert A. M. Stern is Professor of Architecture at Columbia University where he has taught for twenty-five years. Robert A. M. Stern Architects is one of the most significant architectural firms in New York City.

5

Four Decades of Forty Under Forty

1941

William Ballard
Philip G. Barlett
Hamilton Beatty and Alan John Strang
Richard M. Bennett
James Gordon Carr
Robert Carson
Hervey Parke Clark
Alfred Clauss
Memhard N. Culin
Kenneth Day
Howard Dearstine
John Ekin Dinwiddie, Albert Henry Hill,
    and Phillip E. Joseph
Alden B. Dow
Frederick G. Frost, Jr.
John Funk
Percival Goodman
Gruenbaum and Krummeck
William Hamby and George Nelson
Michael M. Hare
Harwell H. Harris
Bernard J. Harrison, Jr.
Don Hatch
Samuel E. Homsey
Caleb Hornbostel
William R. Huntington
Robert Allan Jacobs
Morris Ketchum, Jr.
Carl Kock
George Kosmack
Maynard Lyndon
Willis N. Mills
Murphy & Wischmeyer
Emrich Nicholson and Douglas Maier
Ernest Payer
Geoffrey Platt
Walther Prokosch
Michael L. Roadoslovich
James Irving Raymond
Kenneth H. Rifken
Rodgers & Priestly
Eero Saarinen
Lee Schoen
Paul Schweikher and Robert B. McCombe
Sears & Foote
Esmond Shaw
Richard Boring Snow
Edward Durell Stone
Oscar G. Stonorov
Eastman Studds
Olive F. Tjaden
Ides van der Gracht and Walter Kilham
Paul Luther Wood
Ian Woodner

1966

Anthony Eardley, Peter Eisenman,
    and Michael Graves
Robert Entzeroth and Eric Smith
James Baker
Hobart Betts
Gunnar Birkerts
Cambridge Seven: Louis Bakanowsky,
    Ivan Chermayeff, Peter Chermayeff,
    Alden Christie, Paul Dietrich,
    Thomas Geismar, and Terry Rankine
Lewis Davis and Sam Brody
John Fowler
Charles Gwathmey and Richard Henderson
Hugh Hardy and T. Merrill Prentice, Jr.
William Pedersen, Bradford Tilney,
    Norman Hoberman, Joseph Wasserman,
    and David Beer
Norman Hoberman and Joseph Wasserman
Ben Weese
Thomas J. Holzbog
Peter J. Hoppner
Hugh Newell Jacobsen
George Lewis and T. Merrill Prentice
Mary Otis Stevens McNulty
    and Thomas F. McNulty
Richard Meier
Joseph Merz and Giovanni Pasanella
Robert Mittelstadt
Charles Moore, Donlyn Lyndon,
    William Turnbull,
    and Richard R. Whitaker
Rai Y. Okamoto
Giovanni Pasanella
James Stewart Polshek
David Sellers and William Rainecke,
    and Edwin Owre
Jaquelin T. Robertson
    and Herman Lamaire
Frank Schlesinger
Thomas Vreeland, Jr.
Der Scutt
Werner Seligmann
Robert A. M. Stern
Oliver Lundquist
    and John Jay Stonehill
Stanley Tigerman
Robert Venturi and William Short
John Rauch and Robert Venturi
Thomas Vreeland, Jr.
    and Oscare Newman

1976

D. Agrest & M. Gandelsonas
Emilio Ambasz
Architects in Cahoots
Arquitectonica
Backen, Arrigoni and Ross
Booth and Nagle
Peter de Bretteville
Peter Chermayeff
Chimacoff/Peterson
Stuart Cohen
Dagit/Saylor
Peter L. Gluck
Allan Greenburg
Gwathmey/Siegel
Frances Halsband
Hammond Beeby and Associates
Hardy Holzman Pfeiffer
Hartman/Cox
Peter J. Hoppner
C. Hodgetts and R. Mangurian
Coy Howard
Frank Israel
Etel Thea Kramer
Levinson, Lebowitz, Zaprauskis
Donlyn Lyndon
Andrew MacNair
Machado/Silvetti
Robert Mittelstadt
Potters/Williams
James Volney Righter
Jon Michael Schwarting
Daniel Scully
David Sellers
Robert A. M. Stern
Susana Torre
MLTW/Turnbull Associates
Ueland and Junker
Peter David Waldman
Wells/Koetter/Denis
Timothy Wood

1986

Ace Architects
A2Z
Anderson and Schwartz Architects
Arquitectonica
Ian and Lynn Bader
Wayne Berg
Deborah Berke
Breslin & Mosseri
Carlos Brillembourg
Clark and Menefee Architects
de Bretteville and Polyzoides
Neil M. Denari
Elizabeth Diller
Duany and Plater-Zyberk
1100 Architects
Roger Ferri
Frederick Fisher
Randolph H. Gerner
Paul Haigh
William Hellmuth
Steven Holl
Franklin David Israel
Krueck & Olsen
Daniel Libeskind
Robert S. Livesey
Diane Legge Lohan
Mark Mack
Andrew MacNair
Morphosis
Chien Chung Pei
Robert Quigley
Christopher Rudolph
Stanley Saitowitz
Mark Simon
Alison Sky
John M. Syvertsen
Taft Architects
Billie Tsien
Joseph M. Valerio
Allan Wexler

THE SEARCH FOR NEW TALENT IN 1996

Beverly Russell

Before the 40 UNDER 40 jury – Robert A. M. Stern, Frances Halsband, and Walter Chatham – convened at the Cooper Hewitt National Museum of Design in New York on December 15, 1994, a rigorous search was conducted to find the next generation of candidates. Previous honorees in the lists were canvassed for recommendations. Deans of schools of architecture and design all over the country were tapped for suggestions. This search produced more than 250 names, who were invited to submit their work for consideration. Of these potential candidates, 172 actually sent in portfolios (others on the list were over forty years old, or chose not to enter).

The jury's process of elimination resulted in the fifty-three architects (sixteen women and thirty-seven men) whose work comprises this book. The final list exceeds forty because thirteen partnerships are included, an accepted tradition in the history of competition. Since a book was the

final goal for this 40 UNDER 40 contingent and the production of a book takes roughly a year, the search process began in 1994, geared to a publication date in late 1995 or early 1996, the anniversary year of 40 UNDER 40. With a jury meeting twelve months ahead of publication, the birthdate limitation was therefore established with a little flexibility. The majority of the forty are well under forty in 1996, but one or two who were under forty on the jury date have crossed the birthdate line since then. (This, too, has been consistent in the history of the competition.)

The group was educated at forty-four different universities and they are working in twelve different states: New York (nineteen), California (six), Texas (four), Florida (two), Illinois (two), with Kentucky, Arkansas, Ohio, Connecticut, Massachusetts, New Jersey, and South Carolina each fielding one finalist. Analysts in the architectural profession or academia are bound to notice other characteristics of this group. For example, fourteen of the finalists were either students or are now on the faculty at New York's Columbia University. This statistic is certainly cause for serious commentary. It was a conversation point at the jury meeting, with the adjudicators concurring that New York is the "mecca of meccas" for architecture and design

The 40 UNDER 40 jury at Cooper Hewitt National Design Museum, New York. From left: Robert A. M. Stern, Walter Chatham, and Frances Halsband. All have served as President of the Architectural League of New York. Photograph by H. Durston Saylor.

today. The city attracts people from all over the country and all over the world, and the list demonstrates this cosmopolitan mix. Under the direction of Bernard Tschumi, the current Dean of Architecture at Columbia, the school embraces a very wide range of philosophies – modernist, post-modernist, preservationist, and even deconstructionist – which is part of its magnetism. There is an emphasis on building buildings, which is not so apparent at other educational institutions where discourse and theory reign over the technique of construction. Columbia has taken over as the power center from such former strongholds as Yale, the University of Pennsylvania, the University of California at Berkeley, Harvard, and the Illinois Institute of Technology. Running in second place today is the Southern California Institute of Architecture (SCI-ARC), which has gained its recent momentum through the influence of Los Angeles architect Frank Gehry and his retinue of disciples teaching there.

The West Coast is an influential area for architecture and design, despite what the jury called its "movie mentality" and its geographical location, both of which encourage the culture of destruction, with people moving on and "striking the set," or the earth heaving up and bringing down the walls. As Robert A. M. Stern commented: "If somebody builds an interesting piece of work around New York and then moves on for whatever circumstances, usually the next person buys it because it is an interesting building and they are attracted to it. They make some changes or adjustments, as everybody does, but they don't go and tear it down, which is so often the case in California." Recent earthquakes seem to have led to a fashionable "deconstructed" design approach, which makes a building look as if it is falling apart. The jury rejected most of this "shake and bake" architecture as a cliché. They also criticized a trend toward designing with an architectural checklist of industrial materials including exposed plumbing fittings, distressed steel, birch plywood with exposed rivet heads, floating stairways with tension-wire railings, and other hard-edge aesthetics requiring welding skills. Such assemblages they denounced as "whips and chains and the fetishizing of detailing." Walter Chatham was particularly emphatic about this high-tech tactic, calling it "decadent, and a downgrading of the quality of thought over something that is real and invented and a response to more serious conditions."

The strength of architects from Texas and the Midwest was in their clear preference for building in the vernacular style of the region. The jury felt the vernacular had regained its status as a legitimate source of inspiration. Frances Halsband praised the use of designing to fit the climate, the concept of recycling materials, and other ideas arising from the "green" movement. Walter Chatham commented, however, that he was surprised not to see more concern for ecology. "We can't continue to support our technology and infrastructure given our energy consumption in the world," he pointed out, "yet architects are still designing with single glazing. I think more people would be interested to see designers take mountains of discarded tires or other trash from landfills and make houses from them."

In his 1986 40 UNDER 40 selection, Andrew MacNair organized the entries into four categories: North, South, East, and West. Related very loosely to orientation, West signaled the maverick pioneers working around SCI-ARC; South stood for post-modernism as practiced by Arquitectonica, the movers and shakers in Florida; East distinguished the heavy brigade of the East Coast Establishment; and North alliterated with neo-modernists. As he stated: "Classification is a difficult and often risky undertaking...yet it does help to clarify prevailing tendencies with a time, place and generation." With this final list of 40 UNDER 40 for the

twentieth century, there is no clear direction that hasn't been seen or published before. There is no revolution afoot, no promise of a radical shift in the twenty-first century. The separation of the forty into four groupings — Regional, Modernist, Historicist, and Radical — is a natural occurrence. But there are qualities that deserve attention. Most of the work shown in each category is conspicuous for its real-time, real-world functionality. It may be artful, but it is also friendly and livable. Just as multiculturalism and a plurality of views are accepted in our society today, design options have also broadened. *Inclusive* is the key word. Everything is "in," nothing is excluded, nothing is elusive. Looking back over the decades of 40 UNDER 40 architects and their work, perhaps this evolution of pluralism is the greatest achievement. The general public no longer has to wade through deep architectural discourse to understand what is going on out there in the big world of building. Whether it is an office block, a home, a shop, or an art museum, architecture is more accessible and more aesthetically pleasing than it used to be. As we enter a new millennium, these builders of our universe appear to have learned, grown up, and matured in their art.

FORTY UNDER FORTY REVISITED

40 UNDER 40 evokes a tradition of revolution, a venerable history of more than fifty years of the architects of a younger generation challenging their established elders, changing the rules, making room for something new. This history is both a record of an auspicious beginning and the predictor of a successful career. When the Architectural League of New York mounted the first exhibition of 40 UNDER 40 in 1941, the objective was to present the work of a young generation of architects restlessly waiting in the wings for the end of World War II and the chance to compete with their elders.

In 1966, when Robert A. M. Stern organized the second 40 UNDER 40 for the Architectural League, he described one of his objectives as promoting the importance of Robert Venturi and the Philadelphia School. In 1976, Stern organized another edition of 40 UNDER 40 for *Architecture and Urbanism* magazine in Japan, launching yet another generation – the post-modernists. In 1986, Beverly Russell, then editor in chief of *Interiors* magazine, organized a 40 UNDER 40 that set a new direction. There were eight women on the list, not as tokens but as equals. By that time, in many architecture schools women accounted for almost half of the graduating class and barriers in practice had begun to fall. This current effort, again organized by Beverly Russell, marks the fifth appearance of 40 UNDER 40 and notes another changing of the guard.

What is the fascination of this idea, and why does it continue to reappear? The excitement and challenge of viewing yet another 40 UNDER 40 is in guessing who will develop a successful beginning into a successful career; who will be remembered and who will be forgotten. Looking back, the first 40 UNDER 40 list is remarkable for the number of participants who went on to establish large commercial firms. Eero Saarinen and Edward Durell Stone achieved enormous success and contemporary reputation. Current historians are just beginning to rediscover others on this list: Alden Dow, Harwood Hamilton Harris, Maynard Lyndon, Geoffrey Platt, and Oscar Stonorov among them. Every year brings a new monograph or exhibition of their work. The 1966 group are now quite advanced in their careers, and Stern's selections were prescient. Robert Venturi, Michael Graves, Peter Eisenman, and Richard Meier have proved to be major figures. An extraordinary number of firms in the group – Venturi, Rauch & Scott Brown (now Venturi Scott Brown), Gwathmey Siegel, Hardy Holzman Pfeiffer, The Cambridge Seven, James Stewart Polshek, and Davis Brody – have already won the coveted Firm Award of the American Institute of Architects, a recognition of their continuing professionalism and talent. Changing associations were characteristic of this group. Six appeared in the list twice in two different partnerships. Many in the group have maintained strong connections to academia, with seven serving as deans or chairmen of architecture schools, including Anthony Eardley at the University of Kentucky and now at the University of Toronto; the late Charles Moore, who presided at UCLA, Yale, and the University of Texas, Austin; Donlyn Lyndon at the University of Oregon and MIT; James Stewart Polshek at Columbia; Jaquelin Robertson at the University of Virginia; Werner Seligmann at Syracuse University; Thomes Vreeland at UCLA;

and Stanley Tigerman at the University of Illinois, Chicago.

Focusing on 1976, similar characteristics emerged. At least half the participants devoted considerable time to teaching, and already the group has delivered several deans and department heads, including Tom Beeby at Yale, Susana Torre at Parsons School of Design and now Cranbrook, and Andrew MacNair and myself, who were both at Pratt Institute. The 1976 list was also affected by a major revolution. There were no women included in the 1941 group, and in 1966 only Mary Otis Stevens McNulty appeared. In 1976, however, five women, including myself, were included. We were pioneers. We went to school as the lone women in a class of men and started our careers in a men's world. Diana Agrest, Laurinda Spear, Etel Kramer, Susana Torre, and I have all gone on to practice, to teach, and to pursue responsibilities in public service, combining some "firsts" with continuing careers. Some early bloomers on the 1966 list were still under forty ten years later. Peter Chermayeff, Donlyn Lyndon, and Robert A. M. Stern made their second appearance in 1976, and several firms reappeared thanks to the addition of younger partners. Donlyn Lyndon is unique as the only second generation to make the 40 UNDER 40 list: his father, Maynard Lyndon, was included in the first group in 1941.

The 1986 list differed from earlier ones in that it included young designers in large firms. Perhaps this was a reflection of the building boom and the wealth of the profession at the time. It was not unusual to find a very young designer in a position of great authority doing very large work in a very large firm. Thus the late Roger Ferri was working at Welton Becket; William Hellmuth and Diane Legge Lohan were at Skidmore, Owings and Merrill, Randolph Gerner was at Kohn Pedersen Fox Conway, John Syvertsen was at Hammond Beeby Babka, and Chien Chung Pei was working with his father, I. M. Pei. The academic connection continued with this group, with W .G. Clark chairing the architecture department at the University of Virginia, Elizabeth Plater-Zyberk at the University of Miami, Daniel Libeskind at Cranbrook, and Thom Mayne and Michael Rotondi of Morphosis at SCI-ARC. Again, some of the youngest of the 1976 group managed to make it back for 1986: Laurinda Spear and Bernardo Fort-Brescia of Arquitectonica, Peter de Bretteville, Frank Israel, and Andrew MacNair.

The current edition of 40 UNDER 40, with double the number of women – sixteen – in the group, is welcomed by all of us who have finally passed forty ourselves. It offers a chance to test our skills at clairvoyance and learn from the next generation of architects already in our midst.

Frances Halsband, partner in the New York firm of R. M. Kliment and Frances Halsband, holds the historical distinction of being the first woman president of the Architectural League, the first woman president of the New York Chapter of the American Institute of Architects, and the first woman dean of architecture at Pratt Institute.

REGIONAL

"To find unity in diversity is the role of the seeker of laws. When we find the unity behind the complex array of nature, we find the inherent simplicity of nature and are home in it."

Ralph Waldo Emerson

Frank Lloyd Wright described one of the essential characteristics of what he called organic architecture as natural simplicity. By simplicity, he meant a clean, direct expression, an innate or organic pattern true to its form. Disciples of his spirit and philosophy are very much in evidence today. Regional architecture inherently speaks to the site, the location, and the natural landscape. It does not seek to create a stylistic form derived from personal thought processes, but finds its guidelines directly within the earth, the wind, the climate, the bioregional influences.

In the past decade, with the emergence of "green" architecture, which responds to socially responsible issues of planetary stewardship, the regional architect is coming into the mainstream again. Uniting the land and structure in a sympathetic, complementary composition is a long-established principle. Its revival today demonstrates how time-tested ideas endure and common sense prevails.

Located on a four-acre parcel near Perth, Western Australia, this 2,500-square-foot house won first place in an "Australian Home of the Future" competition. It is oriented toward the north to capture solar gain (in the southern hemisphere, the sun travels across the northern sky). The south-facing rammed earth wall (below) is composed of local iron-rich soils mixed with cement to achieve a reddish brown color. A galvanized- steel energy tower combines an electric wind turbine at top level, solar panels with hot water storage tanks, and two water tanks at different levels for fire prevention. It is sited behind the carport in the entry court (left). A split roof (shown in drawings at right) allows natural light penetration through glass louvers into southern rooms and aids fresh air ventilation through wooden louvers in the northern portion of the house.

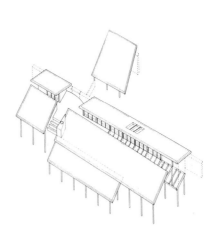

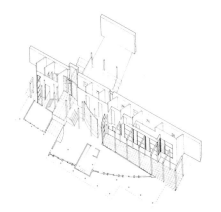

Natural forces

*Her interests coincide with
a maturing awareness of the
wisdom of ecological design*

Kimberly Ackert is a Californian-born globe-trotter with an unusually broad perception of design, gained from living, studying, and working in Denmark, France, Germany, Switzerland, and Australia. In addition to this traveling, as a young honors degree architecture graduate (from California Polytechnic State University), she chalked up important experience with two of the most prestigious architectural firms in New York – Skidmore, Owings & Merrill and Richard Meier & Partners. For these "big league" firms she worked on some blockbuster public buildings, including SOM's Merrill Lynch headquarters in Manhattan and the Citibank tower in Long Island City, and Meier's Ulm Community Center in Germany and Canal + Headquarters in Paris. Her residential design skills were honed in Sydney, Australia, where in 1989 she was invited to become a design partner in a small firm. She stayed three years and was instrumental in the firm's winning two competitions to design and construct residences. The first was a $350,000 "Australian Home of the Future" sponsored by the Monier company in Perth; the other was a $1.5 million, 4,000-square-foot home on the top of a hill overlooking Sydney Harbor, a project that included the interior spaces and some furniture as well as the building.

Ackert's houses combine a basic simplicity in the use of materials with vernacular elements characteristic of Australian architecture and design sensibilities. In a continent that is acutely aware of the rigors of climate, Australians live close to nature and focus on natural givens: sun, shade, wind, and water. Having learned how to incorporate these givens, Ackert is back in the United States at a time when architecture is going "green," and her interests coincide with a maturing awareness of the wisdom of ecological design.

17

A structural steel pergola runs
through the house (above, opposite
lower left), creating an interior
courtyard between the two distinctive
north-and south-facing sides of the
structure. The pergola is integrated
into the interior architecture of the
living room (opposite top), where
it artfully straddles a curving glass
block wall designed to introduce
light from the northern wall. Interior
finishes include corrugated-metal
ceilings (in the dining room, right),
Australian hardwood floors, and
wooden louvers located high
to expel hot air.

This 4,000-square foot residence overlooking Sydney Harbor, Australia, was the owner's first choice in a closed competition between three architectural firms. It is built on a steep slope that drops fifteen feet and has cantilevered terraces on two levels to take advantage of the spectacular view. Entry is on the north facade, with entry stairway on the left and rollup garage door on the right (opposite lower left). Glazing on the upper bedroom floor is shaded with automatic screen devices that are sensor-activated to prevent heat build-up (opposite top left). The main living floor (below) has sliding glass doors out to the pool deck. Axonometric drawings (top left) indicate the linear organization of space. In the upper - floor master bathroom (right) a black granite counter is set on ash veneer cabinets. The sun-scoop ceiling allows hot air to escape through glass louvers.

Eclectic variations

*The power of circumstances
and subtlety of surroundings
define manners and methods*

Jay Baker's background has covered several states. He was born in Omaha, Nebraska, and received a Bachelor of Arts in architecture from Iowa State and a Master of Architecture degree from Rice University, Houston. He has remained in Houston ever since and is a strong influence in architectural activities in the city. In 1990, Baker conceived, designed, and implemented the Light Spikes, Houston's international symbol of welcome for the 1990 Economic Summit of Industrialized Nations. This dramatic visual experience, which combined art and architecture, earned him worldwide attention. As President of the prestigious Rice Design Alliance, Baker organized and managed an international competition for one of the city's parks.

A multidisciplinary designer, Baker has won seventeen local and state awards in architecture, urban design, interior architecture, and graphic design. He has taught at his alma mater as a visiting critic since 1988; his open mind and flexible point of view are well regarded by students. He prefers the lessons of built form to those of dogma and process and believes that the most compelling ideas result from contemporary conditions in a chaotic society. For him, architecture has the ability to create a sense of place even in the most difficult and undesirable circumstances.

23

An existing barn built in Rumson, New Jersey, in 1878 is the subject of an extensive renovation and addition for a family of four. The shell of the original structure has been carefully retained and a new addition placed perpendicular to the original (opposite). The central concern was to renew a barnlike quality in the detailing and massing of the buildings (right).

The interior of the structure was gutted and reorganized (near and far right) to imbue rooms with a rustic feeling. Beams and posts help to enhance the historical associations.

The Bayshore residential development in Tampa, Florida, incorporates thirty-one units and sixty-two automobiles. In an effort to save a stand of 200-year-old oak trees, housing is configured around a central courtyard. Stucco, ceramic tiles, glass block, awning, windows, pipe rails, and vine-covered trellises provide a sense of vernacular community.

To commemorate the
1990 Economic Summit of
Industrialized Nations, held in
Houston, Texas, an array of
eight internally illuminated
columns clad in the translucent
colors of each of the seven
participating nations and the
European Community were
configured against the city
skyline. Each structural
aluminum tube is anchored
to a pier foundation
drilled ten feet deep.

27

Reading the landscape

A Southerner educated at Auburn University, Alabama, where he gained a double bachelor's degree in Architecture and Science in Environmental Design, Marlon Blackwell traveled to Mexico, Guatemala, and Florence, Italy, for further education. In Central America he studied pre-Columbian art and achitecture, and in Italy he earned a Master of Architecture degree.

Pursuing a twin-track career, in 1985 he went to Boston, where he taught at the Boston Architecture Center and worked as a staff architect at CBT Architects. He continued to combine teaching and practice, holding staff positions in the firm of Graham Gund and Payette Associates in Boston while taking on guest critic responsibilities at the Rhode Island School of Design, Roger Williams College, and Syracuse University.

In 1992 he returned to the South, this time to teach at the University of Arkansas and to maintain an independent "after hours" practice in Fayetteville. Blackwell's residential commissions exhibit a sympathetic melding of utility and economy with strong consideration of siting. He is especially artful at harmonizing common materials – particularly

Artful harmonizing of common materials, particularly wood, concrete block, and corrugated metal

wood, concrete block, and corrugated metal – in buildings that are modern yet graceful. He reads the landscape first, mapping his concepts literally from the ground up.

29

Designed as a year-round residence in the mountains of North Carolina, this unusual double-height ultra-size cabin made of mahogany plywood siding with fir battens and tin roof is an interpretation of the ad hoc character of the region's mountain vernacular.

Sited on a natural high-point defined by a granite ridge, the house has the surprise of one massive concrete block wall (above), which acts as the formal edge between the man-made habitat and the wilderness beyond. The house is divided into four distinct parts according to function, each with its own roof, opening onto the central volume (opposite, top and right).

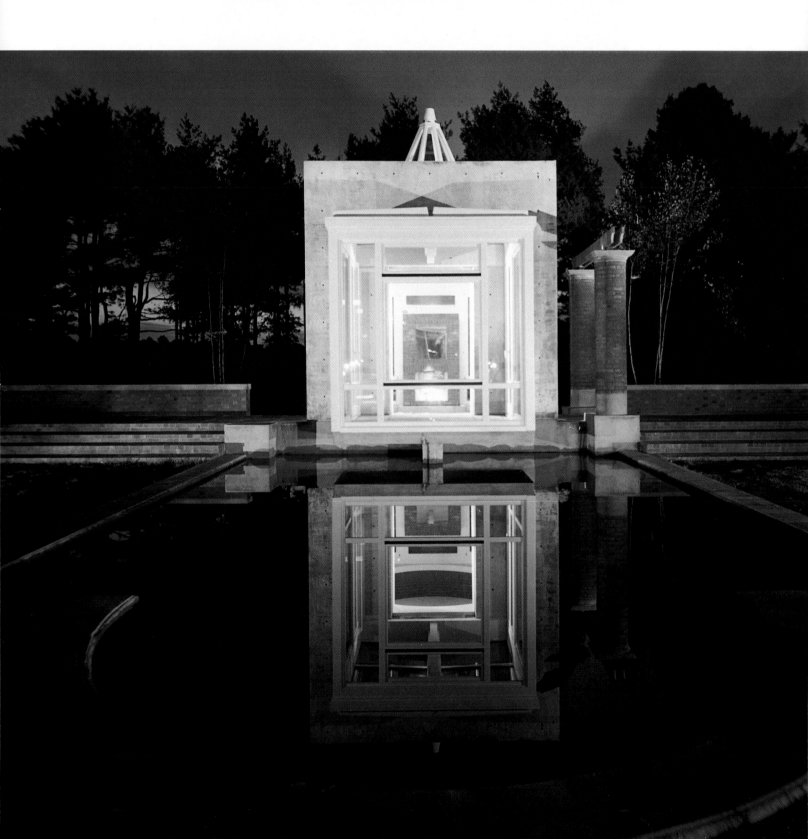

The assignment called for a garden house retreat for quiet contemplation set within a formal garden, to enhance a neoclassical house in Wenham, Massachusetts, and provide an exhibition area for a collection of nineteenth-century sculpture. The design of the garden house is a three-dimensional interpretation of the garden plan, with its linear pool, fountains, arbors, and columns all seeming to melt into the landscape.

In Wedington, Arkansas, a low-cost
hybrid building accommodates
a couple and their two horses, along
with a shop and garage for eight
vehicles. Common materials –
wood, concrete block, and metal –
underscore the utilitarian nature of
the structure. Fencing unites it with
the surrounding horse paddock (left).
The 4,000-square-foot building
was constructed for $40 per square
foot. Operable windows on the second
story take advantage of the prevailing
breeze. A large overhang contributes
shade in summer and allows
low-angled sun to penetrate in
winter. A twelve-foot-wide pole barn
construction system allows for
interchangeable spaces that
accommodate both vehicles
and animals.

Located on a hilltop on the northwestern coast of Sardinia, this villa takes full advantage of the benign climate and the panoramic views. The simplicity and economy of its structure resonate with the vernacular architecture of the Mediterranean, which uses heavy masonry walls to shield the sunlight.

Letting the site speak

*Design that takes into account
locale, history, availability of materials,
construction methods, and
craftsmanship*

Gilles Depardon was born in France and grew up in various European countries as well as Japan. Kathryn Ogawa is of Japanese descent and was born in Los Angeles. Both obtained their undergraduate architectural degrees at the University of Southern California. After further education (Depardon has a Master of Architecture from the Harvard University Graduate School of Design) and working independently for design firms in New York, they established their partnership in 1987, with offices in Manhattan and Rome.

With a background based on a multinational history spanning three continents, Depardon and Ogawa insist that there is more to design than the acts of drawing and designing. In particular, the partners take into account specific issues of locale, history, availability of materials, construction methods, and craftsmanship before making their final decisions. They believe this process produces a dialogue that ultimately leads to a simple yet refined total solution. For them, interior design, furnishings, and detailing are all components in one seamless presentation of harmony and appropriateness, whether embracing small- or large-scale projects, residential or commercial.

37

This villa was designed to be
built by local masons and
craftspeople using traditional
materials and building techniques
that have existed for centuries
(drawing above). The finishing
details incorporate indigenous
climate controls such as carefully
crafted wood shutters, screens, and
pergolas. The house consists of
one basic, large room and three
terraces, each serving different
functions; sliding doors provide
flexibility and privacy.

GILLES DEPARDON
AND KATHRYN OGAWA

Redesigned and reconstructed on the footprint of a residence destroyed by fire in Santa Barbara, California, this small 2,000-square-foot house is compactly organized on two levels (opposite and above). Simple materials reflect budgetary constrictions. The cut-out chair (far right), designed for the Media Lab classroom at the Youth Activity Center of the Los Angeles County Sheriff's Youth Foundation, demonstrates creativity and use of new materials —neoprene and recycled foam—to the students.

Reinventing the way

Environmental factors, sustainable building design concepts, and innovative materials combine with traditional wisdom

A Los Angelino by birth, Robin Donaldson was educated at the University of California at Santa Barbara, where he received a Bachelor of Arts, and SCI-ARC, where he received his Master of Architecture. He began an apprenticeship with Morphosis Architects and worked up to project architect for the firm, working on many award-winning and inter-nationally recognized commercial, institutional, and residential projects. He opened his own office in Santa Barbara in 1989, concentrating on residential and commer-cial works, housing, and furniture design.

Donaldson has an original philosophy – form follows intention – which means that a building is aligned with parameters of budget, site, client needs, and expectations. Although he and his partner, Russell Shubin, do not champion any particular formal or stylistic dogma, they do have a special interest in environmental factors, sustainable building design concepts, and innovative material use and detailing. However, they prefer to explore the ways they operate, believing that this will bring better standards of service to their clients. Reinventing ways of operating, asserts Donaldson, is as important as the built works that actually get accomplished. To this end, Shubin and Donaldson have created a complex web of virtual associations through the computer and are able to interface with other designers and consultants for projects of any size and scale. In this way, they have maximum information and knowl-edge available for input into a particular job.

41

Celebrating the outdoors

Searching for inspiration from natural phenomena that dictate specific design solutions

Ted Flato has gained a national reputation for straightforward regional design that incorporates building forms and materials that are sensitive to the climate. He studied architecture at Stanford University, and began his career in Austin, Texas. He and his partner, David Lake, opened their own firm in San Antonio in 1984 and have won numerous

national, state, and local awards for their work.

From the beginning, Flato steadfastly disregarded "style" trends, searching for inspiration from natural phenomena that dictate specific design solutions. For example, even if a ranch encompasses thousands of acres, according to Flato, "there is only one place to put the house." Where the wind comes from, where the trees stand, where the land rises, and where the sun sets — these are all elements that the pioneers out west understood centuries ago, and they serve as functional yardsticks equally well today. Flato thinks about stone walls, screen porches that face prevailing breezes, and windows that catch the sun as it moves through the day, and even the moon at night. While he celebrates indigenous architecture, there is something inescapably modern about Flato's compositions. His deft assembly of materials gives his work a surprising, sophisticated touch.

On a central Texas ranch with a series of prominent limestone bluffs overlooking the Llano River near Mason, a three-bedroom house takes advantage of the views and breezes, making a strong connection with the outdoors. Massive buttresses were assembled from surface-weathered limestone found at the site.

Designed in a linear plan, the ranch house works with the steep grades and prevailing winds. Flaps constructed of recycled oil field rods are cantilevered from the buttresses to shade the main pavilion as well as the cliffside terraces.

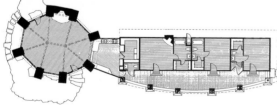

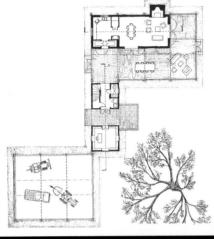

The Carraro ranch house near
Austin, Texas, celebrates the beauty
of indigenous industrial architecture.
The steel frame, with its trusses
and clerestory at the crown of
the roof, was salvaged from a 1920s
factory near Alamo. Metal stairs,
railings, roof vents, bricks, and
other scrap were also recycled into
this three-part residence of
ad hoc assemblages.

On a sand dune in the open grassland of South Texas, the El Tule ranch house rides the landscape with natural ease (above right). While connected to the wide open spaces, it is also a compound enclosing its own contrasting world around a courtyard garden (opposite), where shade trees create a quiet oasis around a central lap pool (right).

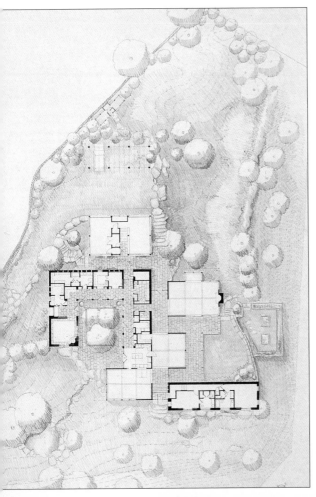

The Lasater house in a residential
neighborhood of Fort Worth, Texas,
overlooks a wide, open river valley.
To take advantage of the natural
characteristics of the site, the design
began with the exterior spaces.
Enclosed courtyards were organized
between a cluster of open pavilions
that look out to the more
distant views (see plan).

Context matters

Linking the building to the site takes precedence, whether in the Napa Valley or the Florida Everglades

Born in Gary, Indiana, Brian Healy went East to study at Pennsylvania State University and the Yale School of Architecture, where he received his Master of Architecture degree. He did his basic training at the offices of Cesar Pelli and Richard Meier, and has combined practical work with academic positions at the American Academy in Rome, the Rhode Island School of Design, Pennsylvania State University, and the University of Virginia. Since 1988 he has based his architecture firm in Cambridge, Massachusetts, working for a variety of clients who appreciate his willingness to subordinate his architectural ideas to their needs.

Despite rigorous attention to the occupants' requirements, Healy always manages to compose one-of-a-kind buildings that respond to their locations, whether in the Napa Valley, the Florida Everglades, or the New Jersey sand dunes, winning design awards in the process. His success led to inclusion of one of his projects in the *Life* magazine article "Houses for Less than $150,000" in June 1994. This sympathetic architect blends a powerful imagination with a practical reality.

A small rustic residence for a horticulturalist in southwest Florida is viewed as a backdrop for the client's interest in plants. The structure is concrete block covered with painted stucco. Windows and jalousies are aluminum.

51

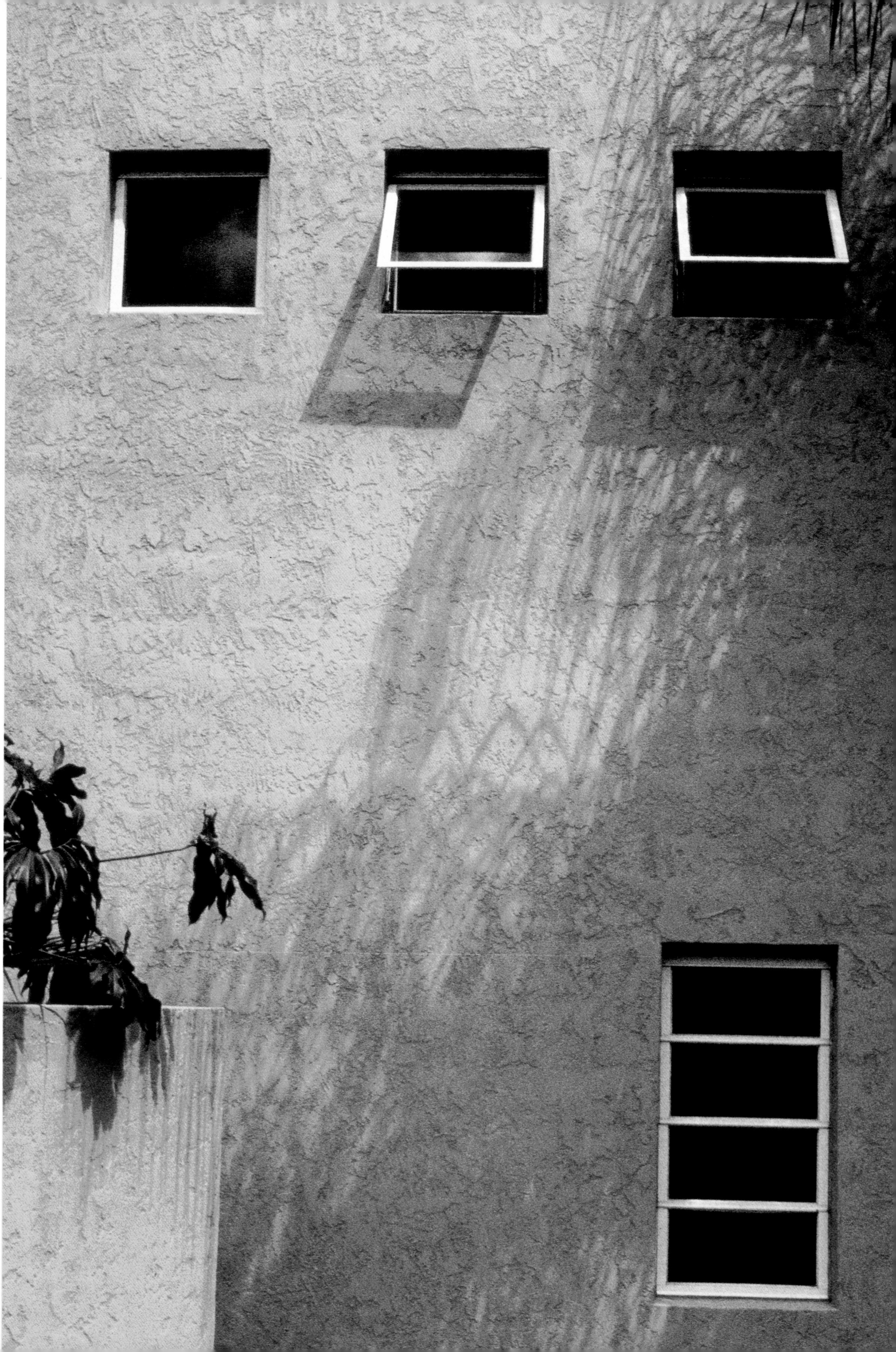

52

BRIAN HEALY

Isolated on a ten-acre tract of palmettos and pines and surrounded by cypress swamps, the house has an organic shape (model below), in keeping with its environment. An exterior court, with tiered planting areas, repeats the curving form (near left).

53

Conceived as an assemblage of parts, this residence in Longport, New Jersey, is located directly on the ocean. The house is wood frame with stucco and cedar walls. The interior surfaces include limestone and mahogany floors. A canopied deck has a pool and entertainment area.

On a corner site where the bulkhead jogs into the bay of Little Egg Harbor, on Long Beach Island, New Jersey, this pavilion-like summer residence rides its nautical locale well and is opened up to make the most of the seaview. The exterior is wood-framed, with cedar siding and fiberglass roof; the interior has birch and terra-cotta floors and mahogany doors that harmonize with the marine display docked around it.

Poetic responses

Integrating a familiar vernacular feeling in the composition of exterior materials, placement of windows, and relationship to the site

Born in Columbus, Mississippi, Whitney Powers went to the University of Mississippi for her undergraduate degree in architecture and then earned a master's in architecture and building design at Columbia University. Despite this interface with the Eastern establishment, Powers has never rejected her Southern origin. This strong rootedness in rural America is reiterated in her poetic writings about her work, in which the sea and coastlines, live oak trees, shrimp and crab, wetlands and the din of insects, the rock and the cloud are all talismans that provoke her creative output.

After paying her dues as an intern in several architectural firms, Powers set up her own office in 1989 in Charleston, South

Carolina. Ever since then, her residential designs – which range from low-cost affordable housing to custom, one-off luxury homes – have caught the eye of national and international critics. She was named among young, promising architects by *Progressive Architecture* in 1990.

When designing a house, Powers integrates a familiar vernacular feeling in her composition of exterior materials, placement of windows, and relationship to the site. Her work conveys a straight-forward understanding of what is required for the fullest enjoyment of cooking, eating, bathing, sleeping, family interaction, and entertainment as well as a preoccupation with capturing sunlight and views. To fulfill these basic living needs, Powers resorts to simple, almost childlike forms and spaces that embody mythic concepts of home.

On Sullivan's Island, South Carolina, adjacent to the U.S. Coast Guard lighthouse, this compound of buildings consists of a main house and two guest pavilions arranged around a swimming pool.

Open white-painted double-height living areas finished with wood give the appropriate rustic feeling.

The character of the original cottage, which was blown away by a hurricane, is retained through vernacular detailing such as the slanted ceiling in the den.

HISTORICIST

"There is a history in all men's lives, figuring the nature of the times deceas'd."

William Shakespeare

King Henry IV , Part II

It is thought that the revival of historical elements and references in architecture and design is part of a search for past glories that may give a sense of stability and order in an increasingly unstable and chaotic society. In the 1980s, what came to be known as the post-modernist style introduced colors, materials, and details – vaulted ceilings, arches, columns, pediments, gold leafing, rusticated stone – from classical architecture, regurgitating them in adaptations rather than authentic representations. This refocusing on history opened up the floodgates to many different eras, broadening the design vocabulary for contemporary architects and designers, many of whom had been educated within a strictly "abstract modern" point of view.

Historicist architects and designers may draw from antiquity, the Renaissance, English vernacular, early modern, or regional Americana for their inspiration. Some are actually engaged in reproducing the past as accurately as possible. They all rejoice in the acceptance of historicist imageries.

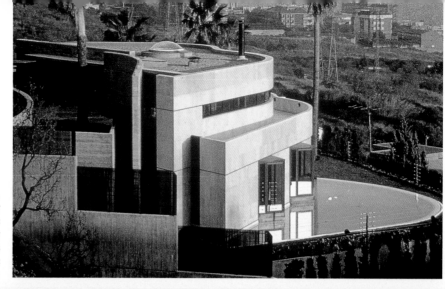

A stark house in Barcelona,
Spain, with forceful masonry
walls articulated in rhythmic
curves, recalls the early history
of modernism and reflects
a mission to create organic
abstract sculpture.

Past reflections

Born in Buenos Aires, Argentina, with American and Italian parents, Victoria Casasco received her first degree, a B.F.A. in sculpture, from the Rhode Island School of Design in 1978. She subsequently received her Master of Architecture at Columbia University in 1983. Her career took off even before she graduated when she became involved with the development and design of the experimental town of Seaside, Florida (with town architects and planners Andres Duany and Elizabeth Plater-Zyberk), and with environmental artist Alan Sonfist. In 1987, after working in the office of Robert A. M. Stern in New York and with Mila Correa Architects in Barcelona, Spain, she returned to Seaside as Town Architect and also began her own practice, Victoria Casasco Studio, based in Venice, California.

A house is not just a house but an addition to a community landscape that everyone sees and enjoys

When given a commission, Casasco's response is to integrate environmental and natural conditions and thus work within the larger cultural and physical context. Local building technologies, site conditions, and economic parameters are the primary elements that determine the final outcome. The process is also likely to include community participation and individual client involvement to ensure a design that is truly compatible with its surrounding needs and program. For Casasco, a house is not just a house but an addition to a community landscape that everyone sees and enjoys.

65

Building code requirements in Seaside, Florida, have been laced together from early Gulf Coast resort community styles, with a dash of English country village vernacular thrown in. In this romantic house complete with viewing tower, the structural frame is exposed in a pleasing arrangement of components that continue as a theme in the interior space.

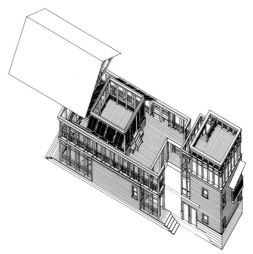

In a complex of village-like pavilions for a family of six in rural New England, a central tower (left) opens below as an entry porch and encloses a glass-walled study above. The reference to historical details occurs both inside and out.

James Childress studied at the Rhode Island School of Design, where he gained his Bachelor of Architecture. In 1970 he joined Moore Grover Harper, now known as Centerbrook, in Essex, Connecticut, one of the most influential East Coast firms for the past three decades. He started out as a project manager and rose to be a principal.

Childress's work has won fourteen national and regional design awards and has been published in numerous architectural magazines and books. What makes Centerbrook an ongoing subject of recognition and discussion is the firm's approach to design. Neither strictly "modern" nor "post-modern" in its style, Centerbrook pursues an

idiom born out of its late principal Charles Moore's viewpoint that architecture should be "fun" and easily understood by the layperson. Moore believed that the architect's first obligation is to create a building that provides emotional sensations in its design and interiors. For this reason, Centerbrook's work – whether large-scale structures for schools and corporations or small-scale private houses – incorporates well-known and familiar elements that evoke strong emotional responses and often reflect an amalgam of American architectural history. For example, a house may have curved roofs and dormers, arched windows, Gothic touches, stone walls, or vertical barn-style

battening; the structure is at once old and new, an invention made of traditional elements. It settles comfortably into the landscape from a distance, but close up comes alive with animated color and detail. Inside, sociability, whimsy, and surprises of light make the rooms feel comfortable and livable.

Messages with meaning

Sociability, whimsy, and surprises of light make the rooms feel comfortable and livable

A pair of pavilions, each with chimneys of different sizes and angles, are joined by a vestibule to make a picturesque composition in the Connecticut hills (above and opposite). Silk ceiling draperies hide lights to give subtle illumination in the living room (top).

A dark, rambling bungalow on the Connecticut shore required a modest renovation. By extending wood beams across the living room to the outside and adding a window wall (left), views from the living room are expanded to capture a Japanese garden.

A dialogue with time and nature

Passion, joy, and commitment to the art of building

Although Jorge Hernandez is a Cuban expatriate who has lived in Florida most of his life, he believes that the physical presence of Havana, with its robust architecture, brilliant light and color, made an impression on him at a very early age. After two years at a liberal arts college in Alabama, he decided to major in architecture at the University of Miami. Upon graduation, he combined graduate teaching with a private practice; his first commission was published in *Architectural Record*.

Hernandez has continued to teach and build ever since, and his work has been shown in numerous publications, from serious architecture journals to popular newspapers and magazines. What sets his work apart is his "passion, joy, and commitment" to the art of building, which he feels is an enduring dialogue between mankind, time, and nature. Environmental sensitivity is paramount and, is beautifully expressed in the private houses he has designed in his locality. The author of several books, Hernandez is researching the Mediterranean Revival houses of Coral Gables, which are an ongoing inspiration to him in his current work.

73

The Villa Gutierrez is an imposing waterfront residence in Miami, celebrating what the architect calls "protoclassical or archaic freedom before the coming of Hellenistic Miami." The two columns in the portico (painted the red of a tropical fruit called a mamey) are rotated, tapered piers. The main living room (opposite and right) has a great demi-lune window overlooking the sea.

With an intentional hint toward Venetian palazzo style, the Villa Pou is located at the perpendicular junction of two canals that give way to the ocean in Miami. A symmetrical facade on the street contrasts with a more varied and picturesque facade at the back overlooking the waterfront (opposite). The tower, containing the morning room and master bedroom, is extended at its base by the pool, which engages the canals.

Resembling the garden casino of a grand mansion, La Tamarindo is a villa on the smallest buildable lot size in Coral Gables, Florida. The downstairs consists of two large rooms – a formal room to the front (left and right) and a family room at the back. Upstairs are three bedrooms and two bathrooms. A stone-floored pergola-covered terrace serves as an additional outdoor living space in this semitropical environment.

In this pastel watercolor of
Tres Villas, architect Jorge Hernandez
depicts the front facades of all three
of his buildings: the Villa Pou, La
Tamarindo, and the Villa Gutierrez.

78

TRES

The Villa Don Giovanni project adds Mozart's famous opera to the repertoire of mythic texts used as raw material for architectural exploration. The villa (opposite) is set in an imaginary Venetian landscape. The commendatore's house (right) is of medieval origins.

80

The studiolo articulating desk with its lyre base (left) and the pilaster bookcase with an original Mayernik relief carving bring the beauty of history into the present.

Allegory and humanism

Fully conscious of the issues that classically grounded work raises, he feels a need for the renaissance of humanism

In a world of electronic media, space stations, and rock stars, the work of David T. Mayernik belongs to another century. He is an architect, urban designer, and fresco painter in the classical manner. He graduated with a Bachelor of Architecture from the University of Notre Dame and spent his third year abroad in Rome, an experience that took him back to his family's roots in Italy, where his grandfather had worked as a stone mason in the Veneto region.

Returning to Rome in 1988 as a fellow of the American Academy in Rome, Mayernik produced over forty sketches of sites in Rome and Italy and pursued his studies of fresco painting. Mayernik's uncanny ability in rendering exquisite drawings and watercolors and his keen devotion to historic architecture was quickly noted by his peers. Between 1983 and 1994 he worked for a number of distinguished architectural firms on assignments involving historic national buildings such as the Art Institute of Chicago, the Riggs Bank, Deerfield Academy, and the Brooklyn Museum. In addition, he was appointed project designer and architect for a number of residences and estates in Connecticut, Colorado, and Palm Beach.

Mayernik now maintains an independent practice in Brooklyn Heights, New York, and his roster of projects reflects his artistic strength. He has worked on painting commissions for clients in Philadelphia, New York, Vienna, and Rome. He designed a banner and completed a fresco for the American Academy in Rome and is also working on a Second Century Founder's Memorial for the institution. The financial investment company Bear Stearns commissioned him to design a conference table. The city of St. Paul commissioned him to design new urban bridges and to work on the Minnesota Capitol Area with his partner, Thomas Rajkovich – a project that elicited controversial reactions about the future of the American city.

Fully conscious of the issues that his classically grounded work raises, Mayernik lectures and writes on allegory in the urban realm and the need for a renaissance of humanism rather than a mere revival of classicism and tradition.

81

The addition of a classical portico to an existing brick residence in Lake Forest, Illinois (shown before renovation, opposite), celebrates the arrival at a grand house. The entire portico is crafted in wood, with copper roofing, and rests on a concrete foundation and steps. Pear trees are positioned to frame the portico from the approach drive, and a manicured hedge creates an entrance court.

Respect for times gone by

The comfort and reassurance of distant origins in a world of contemporary chaos

Thomas Norman Rajkovich carries the banner of classical architecture in the Midwest. Rajkovich attended the University of Notre Dame, where he graduated with a Bachelor of Architecture. After winning the Chicago Architectural Club's Burnham Prize for independent study, he went to Rome; since then he has found little inspiration in contemporaneity. His drawings, his ideas, his beliefs are steeped in historic precedent, which he pursues with a passion. The noted Chicago architect Stanley Tigerman has described Rajkovich's connoisseurship and his concern with proportion and detailing as "extraordinary."

Fine-tuning his training at the offices of Christopher H. Rudolph and Hammond, Beeby and Babka in Chicago (followers of European architectural precedent), Rajkovich opened his own office in Evanston, Illinois, in 1986. He lectures, teaches, and practices what he calls "the art of proper building," explaining the intricacies of the classical language to audiences and clients who seek the comfort and reassurance of distant origins in a world of contemporary chaos. Recent projects include a proposal for the Korean War Veterans Memorial in Washington, D.C., an enhancement of Grant Park in Chicago, and a civic enhancement project for Beverly Hills. He is the winner with David Mayernik of the international competition for the design of the Minnesota State Capitol grounds, a project covering thirty-six acres and one of the largest proposed formal public gardens of this century.

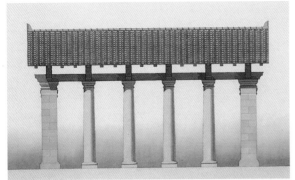

Detail of one of four arched gateways proposed as an enhancement for the Buckingham Fountain terrace in Grant Park, Chicago (opposite). The iconography of the classical gateways records the events represented by the four stars on the flag of the City of Chicago: the Fort Dearborn Massacre, the Great Fire, the World's Columbian Exposition, and the Century of Progress International Exposition.

A proposed market loggia for a park in Evanston, Illinois, is composed of fundamental elements of architecture: column and beam, wall and arch, and roof. The proportions are regulated by harmonic consonances. Articulated with a bird beak molding, the trusses take the triangulated form of a bird in flight.

Harmony by design

Drawing on historical ideas of proportion and ornament from classical traditions

When Charles Warren decided to pursue his graduate degree in architecture at Columbia University in 1976, he found a professor and mentor who was to guide his career for the next decade: Robert A. M. Stern. In the early 1970s Stern was among the growing group of New York architects embracing post-modernism, advocating a return to ornament and decoration, a reconnection with architectural history, and a continuity with tradition. He stood firmly against the belief that modern technology inevitably gives rise to a universal, industrial style of building.

Immediately upon graduation, Warren joined the Stern office and was responsible for the design and execution of a wide variety of projects, including public buildings, residences, and competitions between 1979 and 1982 and subsequently between 1984 and 1987. Stern's reintroduction of the Shingle Style, a hybrid of classical and vernacular elements but in contemporary variations, and his insistence that the past offered standards for the future, was music to Warren's ears. In 1986 Warren set up his own independent architectural office in Manhattan and continued to borrow and adapt classical themes in his residential work, often using the proportions of the golden section to orchestrate harmony throughout his buildings. Having established his reputation as a traditionalist, in 1990 he was appointed Town Architect of Seaside, Florida, in charge of administration of the code and design reviews of the eighty-acre planned resort community on the Gulf Coast that emulates the best qualities of nineteenth-century southern town planning. Warren was able to bring his own special talents to bear on the Seaside Post Office, a small but important building which through its design and materials evokes the memory of small-town civic life.

87

Like an ancient Roman villa, the Red House at Seaside, Florida, is arranged with specific orientations to the sun, the sea, and the windows. The design and ornament are orchestrated to lead upward from a simple entry to the Tuscan pavilion at the top.

CHARLES WARREN

With proportions based on
the harmonic ratios of the golden
section, each room, both indoors
and out, forms part of a sequence of
unfolding visual experiences. All
the details – beams, rafters, columns,
doors, and windows – are used
to make explicit connections to the
architectural traditions of Greece
and Rome. From the colonnaded
pinnacle, views capture the
dunes and sea.

On the shore of Lake Michigan, bordered by a pine forest, this house responds to two very different landscapes. On the lake side, large windows and raised decks command views and broad steps cascade down to the sand. In sharp contrast, the intimacy of the garden interfaces with the woods beyond.

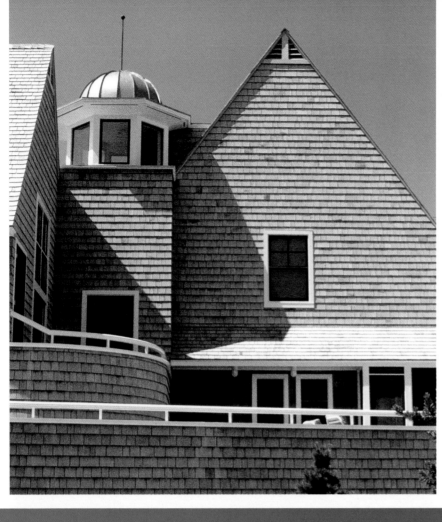

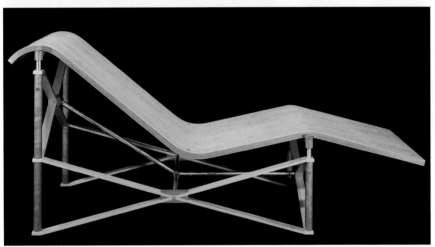

Table and chaise longue (left) are part of a series of wood and metal furniture.

The main floor of the Lake Michigan house (left) is raised to provide views across the dunes. Stairs ascend to the master bedroom (opposite) and then to the guest bedrooms and on up to the observation tower.

MODERNIST

"Modern life demands, and is waiting for, a new kind of plan, both for the house and for the city."

Le Corbusier

Towards a New Architecture,
first published in 1927

At the beginning of this century, industrialization moved into high gear. Thousands of inventions patented in the nineteenth century were implemented to create a new spirit in society. The automobile, the transatlantic liner, and the first airplanes made regional and international travel possible on a previously unimaginable scale. Architecture and design broke from custom and tradition. Le Corbusier conceived the machine for living in, with baths, sun, hot and cold water, warmth at will, conservation of food, hygiene, and beauty all regulated through a sense of good proportion and modern technology. The flowing open spaces of modern houses with streamlined, built-in, and pared-down furnishings matched the new liberated sociocultural attitudes: votes for women, women in the work force, home appliances instead of servants.

Modern conveniences and modern design flourish today in a fast-paced civilization that is oriented to doing everything better, quicker, easier. Reductive design makes life simpler and less complicated.

Industrial elegance

*Transfor-
mations of
interior spaces
to meet the
functions of
today*

Although he was born in
Boulder, Colorado, Stan
Allen's destiny has been in
the East since he first went
to Brown University, and
later to the Cooper Union,
New York, and Princeton
University, where he
received his Master of
Architecture degree.
Throughout his developing
career, he has combined
academic activities as a
visiting critic and lecturer
with architectural writings,
exhibition installation, and
design practice – an
unusually comprehensive
commitment that attests to
his intellectual strength
and creative talent. Along
the way, he has picked up
numerous awards and
fellowships. He was winner
of the Young Architect's
Forum at the Architectural
League of New York in
1988; gained a fellowship
in architecture from the

New York Foundation for
the Arts in 1990; and
received project grants from
the National Endowment
for the Arts in 1991 and the
New York State Council on
the Arts in 1992. His work
has been published in a
range of magazines, books,
and theoretical papers.

After working in the
offices of three significant
architectural firms, Agrest
and Gandelsonas and

Richard Meier & Partners
in New York, and Rafael
Moneo in Madrid, between
1978 and 1987, Allen
moved into academia,
teaching first at the Rhode
Island School of Design
and then at the Harvard
Graduate School of Design,
Columbia University, and
the Royal Danish Academy
of Art. In 1990 he opened
his own studio in New York
while continuing to teach

at Columbia University
as an assistant professor of
architecture.

In addition to interior
renovations, his work
includes design and
construction of galleries for
contemporary art. Owners of
Manhattan loft residences,
where wide-open spaces
demand clever organization
and judicious architectural
intervention, enjoy the fruits
of his creative ability.

97

Intricate trussing and
penetration of light characterize
the computer laboratory at
Columbia University.

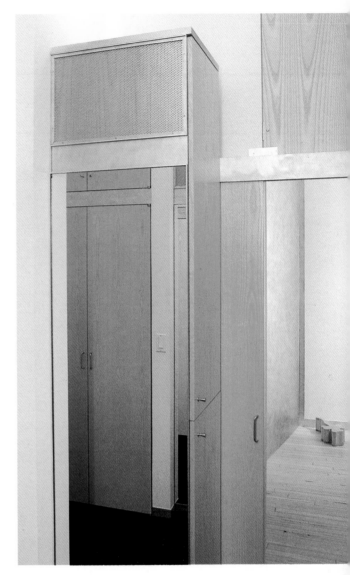

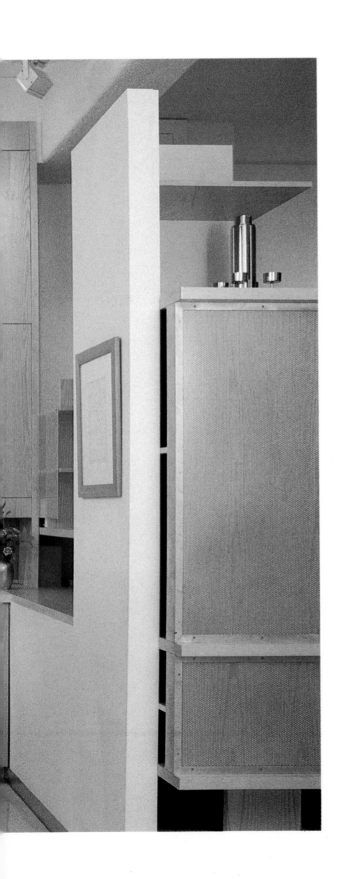

A Manhattan loft renovation for an
art collector and gallery director is
an orchestration of connected spaces,
with a repetition of materials – wood,
marble, and steel – creating a
coordinated theme.

Shamana, a small
fifteen-by-twenty-foot retail store
in Manhattan selling art to wear, is
grandly conceived as both a public
plaza and a precious jewelry box. The
iconography of the shop is derived
from the nature of the objects on
show and shamanic themes. Critical
elements include twenty-one hand-
made light fixtures, four movable
steel display cases, two walls of
nails, and a large golden crown.
The ingenious project received an
award for interior design from
the New York Chapter of the
American Institute of Architects.

Symbolic studies

Mojdeh Baratloo and Clifton Balch met at the University of Michigan in 1978 while working on their Master of Architecture degrees, and have been collaborating on design projects ever since. Baratloo gained experience in the New York offices of Eli Attia and Todd Williams and Billie Tsien, while Balch worked for Gunnar Birkerts and Mitchell/Giurgola. Baratloo-Balch Architects became a formal partnership in 1984, with offices in Manhattan. Both partners teach consistently and have been associated with Harvard, Columbia, and Cornell Universities, as well as the Rhode Island School of Design and Parsons School of Design.

Baratloo and Balch are an energetic team working in a variety of artistic disciplines, including residential, commercial, and public architecture, exhibition design, landscape design, furniture design, and theoretical studies. They have also collaborated with other artists on sets for performance and on urban enhancement projects. They are particularly concerned about the deteriorating industrial infrastructure and what can be done to transform blighted conditions. A quality of thoughtfulness pervades all their work. Symbolism and imagery are the guiding factors, whether they are designing a retail store, an exhibit, a park, or a residence. They have won awards and fellowships from the American Institute of Architects and the New York Foundation for the Arts.

An energetic team working in a variety of artistic disciplines

101

Grounded in the tradition of New England, this Connecticut Island house is an articulation of individual lodgings for each function: pool house (right and below), car house, guest house, and larger living house. The architecture of regional wood churches, the surrounding barns, and early sloped-roof colonial houses provided inspiration.

A distinctive, rigorously modern aesthetic gives their work a unique signature

Refining principles

Karen Bausman and Leslie Gill met while undergraduates at the Cooper Union, New York, where they both gained their Bachelor of Architecture degrees. After graduating, they joined forces as partners and opened their own firm in Manhattan. (After thirteen years, they disbanded their partnership in January 1995 – following the 40 UNDER 40 jury process – when Bausman went to study in Italy on a fellowship from the American Academy in Rome.) Right from the beginning, they were recipients of prizes and awards and were included in group shows of promising young architects. The most prestigious universities sought both of them out as visiting critics or adjunct professors – Yale, Princeton, Parsons School of Design, McGill, Columbia. Rather than following a designated style, they have created a distinctive, rigorously modern aesthetic that gives their work a unique signature.

Within the context of a professional practice and academic appointments, Bausman and Gill have explored the boundaries of architecture, pushing the envelope of interiors and exteriors for a wide variety of clients. They have tackled shops and offices for high-profile organizations such as Warner Bros., Drenttel Doyle Partners, and Sonia Rykiel, as well as residential commissions for houses, lofts, and apartments. In between these projects, they have also focused on furniture, wall reliefs, and other artistic efforts of a more theoretical nature.

These two forceful and multitalented designers represent a new generation of women who have won their place at the top in a traditionally male-dominated field.

105

This two-story house on
Long Island Sound responds to
the small caretaker's cottage it abuts.
The Arts and Crafts vernacular has
been translated into a modern
aesthetic that continues to respect the
use of natural materials, both
inside and out.

The offices of Warner Bros. Records in Rockefeller Center, New York, celebrate the creative individual internalized within an American corporate hierarchy. The offices' emptiness is intentionally designed to allow the spectator to participate actively.

Two different investigations into visual acuity. An optometric store (top left and left) responds to the science and craft of optics. The screens (above) are part of a series of personalized visions.

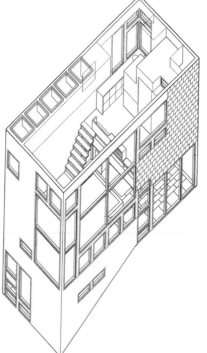

This 900-square-foot residence at Todds Point, Kentucky, uses the constraints of the program and budget as opportunities to exploit the qualities of the landscape. The artistic, geometrical arrangement of wood and glass sets a new standard in low-cost housing.

Rooms with a view

Investigating the relationships within the landscape, between the ground, trees, and sky

A Chicagoan by birth, David M. Biagi won honors as an outstanding graduate at the University of Kentucky and went on to be the highest-ranking graduate at Ohio State University, where he gained his Master of Architecture degree and an American Institute of Architects medal. He went East, where he worked in the high-profile offices of Eisenman Robertson and Gwathmey Siegel in New York. There he worked on projects from Knoll furniture designs to Disney golf clubs and a residence for media magnate David Geffen, before returning to Shelbyville, Kentucky, to set up his own independent practice in 1992.

Living in rural America gives him the opportunity to investigate the relationships within the landscape, between the ground, trees, and sky. He seeks to dissolve the boundaries between the man-made and the site and achieve a harmonious interactive discourse between these two elements. His work also addresses the constraints of a generation working in leaner times when affluence has been replaced by economy. Using standard building products and materials, Biagi brought construction costs down to $45,000 for a 900-square-foot home in the Kentucky farmlands for a young couple. Framing the landscape from multiple vantage points, it is a triumphant result of everything he has learned to date about the complex relationships that go into a building.

KIM COLEMAN
AND MARK CIGOLLE

Micro meets macro

Using computer technology to get away from preconceived notions in architecture and lead to significant transformations

Kim Coleman and Mark Cigolle are based in Santa Monica, California, on the Pacific Rim where East meets West and technology drives megabillion industries. Both came to the West from educational and working experiences in the East. Cigolle, a graduate of Princeton and Harvard, worked for a constellation of superstars, including Michael Graves, I. M. Pei, Richard Meier, and Peter Eisenman, before setting up his own office in New York in 1977. Coleman obtained her Master of Architecture degree from the University of Virginia. They established their California partnership in 1982. Both have concurrently had teaching positions at the University of Southern California School of Architecture, where Coleman is an assistant professor and Cigolle has been a visiting associate professor.

Cigolle and Coleman have been instrumental in developing design studies that integrate the computer into the design process. Rather than utilizing the technology as a tool for replicating conventional techniques, they attempt to engage the computer in the formative stages of a design idea. Understood as a tool for experimentation, Coleman insists, the computer helps to generate alternatives and leads to significant transformations. The underlying intent is to get away from preconceived notions in architecture and building and to let the computer realize true innovation.

111

The architects' own residence in Santa Monica, California, explores the duality of a house for living and working. It is sited on a steep canyon slope and comprises two sections, a tower for living and work activities, and a block that serves multiple needs: garage, children's play, and entertainment areas.

KIM COLEMAN
AND MARK CIGOLLE

A family of forms makes
up the studio house, presenting
a purposefully disparate set of
variations in materials. The complex
orchestration symbolizes the range
of experiences and activities within.
The house is a self-contained environment that includes places for peaceful
contemplation as well as studios and
offices for work and rooms for
vibrant family interaction.

KATHRYN DEAN
AND CHARLES WOLF

Landscapes of the mind

An emphasis on spaces and interiors, creating views and places for quietness and reflection

Kathryn Dean and Charles Wolf met at graduate school in the early 1980s at the University of Oregon. They were much influenced by teachers who had studied and worked with the master architect Louis Kahn, an experience that instilled an appreciation for material presence and strong order in their work. After studying on fellowships at the American Academy in Rome, they returned to New York and established their own firm in 1991. Recognition came quickly. They were winners of the Progressive Architecture Young Architects Competition and the Architecture Discovery Competition. Their first project for housing won an American Institute of Architects award; another house was chosen for a Concrete Institute Award.

Dean and Wolf have developed a very specific philosophy in their work. They believe that building is a marriage of the landscape of man, which they interpret as mind and thought, and the landscape of earth, which is concerned with sensual feeling. Both are necessary for a full experience of life, they say, and every project they undertake has shades of each. They put a lot of emphasis on spaces and interiors, creating views and places for quietness and reflection. Equally important are the physical sensations enjoyed when moving through a space — looking, touching, walking. By excavating the polarities of opposites and contradictions, they hope to arrive at an ultimately harmonious destination.

115

A painter's viewing studio (left) belongs to a tripartite set of buildings in which work is presented as sequences of experiences (see overleaf).

The garden terrace of this house (above) became the family library (left) through extension and expansion, its anchoring hearth providing a haven for conversation.

Three work spaces
accommodate the needs
of a process-oriented
painter who lives in a
suburban environment.
The organization seeks to
create layers by extending
the sequence of movement
from the rough work area,
with its storage of tools
and equipment, to the
finished painting studio,
with its skylit roof.

KATHRYN DEAN
AND CHARLES WOLF

119

In the depths of the woods, a
country house connects earth with sky
in vertical expanses of glass.

Anchored to the edge of a dramatic thirty-foot sheer drop of rock formation, this house begins as a wall and steadily rises in a spiraling motion that culminates in the entry court.

KATHRYN DEAN
AND CHARLES WOLF

To organize a 3,800-square-foot Manhattan industrial loft space into a functional place for living, a major division was created with a forty-eight-foot-long raw steel and glass wall. This establishes the boundaries of master bedroom and bath area from the rest of the apartment. It is partially sandblasted for privacy, and a curtain controls the clear glass (opposite, below) to allow the entire space to be as a whole.

Exploring a narrative

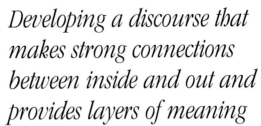

Developing a discourse that makes strong connections between inside and out and provides layers of meaning

Tom Hanrahan and Victoria Meyers met at Harvard University while studying for their Master of Architecture degrees and subsequently established their New York office together. Active participants in the Manhattan architectural scene, they were named among the Architectural League's Young Architects in 1986 and Emerging Voices in 1992. With more than a dozen awards to their credit by 1992, they entered a prestigious competition to design the headquarters of the American Institute of Architects offices in New York City. Their first-place design finished construction in 1993.

Hanrahan and Meyers's projects reflect the idea that it is the continuing transformation of urban structure that characterizes modern life. Thus, when beginning a project, they evaluate the streetscape and the building exterior, using this information as the basis for their interior design. In this way, a narrative discourse evolves that makes strong connections between inside and out and provides layers of meaning within the project. This fundamental approach is applied to diverse programs and many scales.

JOHN KEENEN
AND TERENCE RILEY

Revealing history

*This architectural team is
preoccupied with juxtapositions
of old and new and the way
things go together*

John Keenen and Terence Riley met while students at Columbia University School of Architecture, where they both gained their master's degrees. They worked independently for other distinguished architectural offices before setting up their partnership in 1984. With a strong interest in European history, they have taught at schools in Germany, and in 1988 and 1991 they participated in the Andrea Palladio competition in Vicenza, Italy, both times winning a citation for their work. According to Keenen, the two architects have been most influenced by Italian architect Carlos Scarpa, whose masterly techniques of joining new additions to old historical structures in Italy gave them special insights. They were able to apply these insights to residential projects that involved restoring and adding to existing structures.

As Chief Curator of the Department of Architecture and Design at the Museum of Modern Art in New York since 1991, Riley pursues a full-time job organizing important exhibitions and writing and editing books that accompany them. His interaction in the design partnership is ongoing, however, and he is fully engaged in a consulting capacity in the work going through the office.

Keenen and Riley have received notable distinctions and honors. They were named as Emerging Voices by the Architecture League of New York in 1990. They received a New York Foundation for the Arts fellowship award in 1991. They were finalists in the major international competition organized by the Cathedral of St. John the Divine in New York to produce a design for the completion of the cathedral. Keenen declares that the firm's current goals are to embrace the larger public realm with their work. Their first major project in this area is a hospice for the terminally ill in New Jersey, commissioned by a private-sector client with a non-profit organization.

125

The owners of a weekend country house in Lambertville, New Jersey, wanted an additional place for entertainment (playing pool, dancing, listening to music) away from their main residence. The ruins of an eighteenth-century millhouse on the property, with walls of two-foot-thick stone, provided the foundation for the new "casino." A clerestory runs almost continuously around the building to bring in light (right), and its dividing metal posts provide the support for the concrete slab and railings for the new terrace and screened pavilion above.

New construction containing a
kitchen and other services was added
to the lower level of the casino, now
the major entertainment space, with
its pool table and bookshelves. This
addition supports a walkway leading
to the upper terrace (left). The roof of
the screened pavilion (opposite
below) is metal over a curved marine
plywood subsurface.

Previously the servants' quarters,
the top floor of a turn-of-the-century
Georgian-style house was transformed
into a screening room for the
twentieth century. A shallow barrel-
vaulted ceiling was inserted into a
space with no architectural detailing
and concealed valance lighting was
installed at the edges of the vault.

The floor is stepped to provide optimal
viewing of the screen. A built-in leather
sofa marks the upper level of the room,
while individual armchairs provide
additional seating on the two lower
tiers. Silk-covered walls, aesthetically
pleasing and in keeping with the house,
also contribute acoustical properties.

In an Upper West Side Manhattan apartment where there is no view, an internal vista was created with a visual path that provides views of the entire space. Horizontal slots are cut into architectural elements, and built-in cabinets at standing and sitting heights help to create private panoramas.

Virtual and actual

*They believe the oscillations of
the cyberworld will unbundle
traditional assumptions*

Sulan Kolatan and William
MacDonald bring a wide,
global view to their
partnership. She was born
in Turkey and studied
in Germany. He is from
Massachusetts and
studied at the Architectural
Association in London
and the Berlin Summer
Academy for Architecture.
They both earned graduate
degrees in architecture
at Columbia University and
now both teach there,
with their firm's offices
(established in 1986) just
around the corner.
Although they enjoy the
constant philosophical
discourse that academic life
offers, they feel it is very
important to practice as
well. The explorations and
discoveries they make
in actually working on a
project regenerate their
energy in the classroom.

Kolatan and
MacDonald were named in
the third and fifth Young
Architects Forum and
identified as Emerging
Voices by the Architectural
League in 1992. In their
renovations of New York
apartments and loft spaces,
they like to emphasize
the deeper relationships of
entry, corridors, living and
sleeping spaces, explaining
that "a room is more than
a space divided by walls."
With an intelligent eye on
the future, Kolatan and
MacDonald believe keeping
in step with electronic
technology will be crucial.
The oscillations of the
cyberworld will unbundle
traditional assumptions,
provoking change in many
areas. They cite shopping
malls, airports, museums,
corporate offices, and Third
World countries as places
where tuned-in designers
will find abundant
opportunities to experiment
with virtual and actual
reality in the twenty-first
century.

129

SULAN KOLATAN
AND WILLIAM MACDONALD

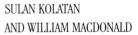

An aluminum wall running almost the entire length of this loft in Manhattan's Chelsea district serves as a divider, a storage unit, and a display device for the occupants' considerable art collection. The use of mirror and glass walls and shelving introduces a sense of ambiguity between virtual and actual. All of these components have a practical value. When the occupants move, the walls and glass panels can be taken down and reconfigured with bolted connections to their new needs. Their traces will be completely erased from the loft, which will be left in its original state.

A Manhattan loft for a couple with three children explores the flexibility of a home that adjusts to changing lifestyles. Three sliding panels (below) divide formal and informal spaces. Another panel, perpendicular to the three, partitions a study from the formal living area. Three pivoting doors (right) establish a connection between the study and the master bedroom.

SCOTT MARBLE
AND KAREN FAIRBANKS

Establishing relationships

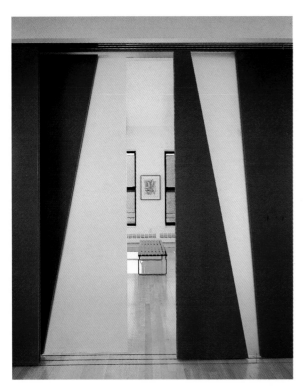

Karen Fairbanks and Scott Marble launched their New York firm in 1990, after being principals in separate firms. They maintain a close association with Columbia University, where they both received their master's degrees in architecture. Marble is an adjunct professor and Fairbanks is Program Director of the undergraduate architecture program.

Marble and Fairbanks made their mark as a design team very quickly. They were selected as one of five finalists from over 600 submissions in a worldwide competition for the Nara Convention Hall International Design Competition in Japan. Their blue building with a glass facade incorporated five huge video screens that could project events taking place inside the

building or around the world. Although it was not the winning design, their project received international publicity. Engaged with ideas about the global economy and a world culture linked through communications technology, Marble and Fairbanks nevertheless concentrate on existing rather than virtual conditions. They see their design work as being practical rather than utopian, and they strive to cement specific relationships in the context of the continuum of history.

Bringing together new and existing ideas to make architecture and design more friendly

133

Latin rhythms

Having traveled extensively in Mexico as a child, he recalls the influences of tropical landscapes, ruins, and strong modern architecture

Born in Los Angeles, with a Scandinavian-American mother and a Mexican father, Mark Rios traveled extensively in Mexico as a child and recalls the influences of tropical landscapes, ruins, and strong modern architecture. He did undergraduate study in architecture at the University of Southern California and then went to Harvard, where he graduated with two master's degrees – in architecture and landscape architecture. As president of his own twelve-person firm in Los Angeles, Rios strives for a multidisciplinary approach and has successfully tackled a wide range of projects, from children's furniture to private gardens, major municipal facilities, and residences for prominent Hollywood personalities. This mix of activity, he believes, keeps ideas fresh and the mind open.

Rios's Latin-influenced flair for color has made him particularly adept at child care centers where his uninhibited palettes create happy places for youngsters. Universal, Disney, and Warner Bros. have all turned to him for their corporate child care facilities, which are considered part of the responsibility of running film studios and media empires in Hollywood today. Rios could have given all his clients variations of the same theme, but instead he prefers to take each as an individual challenge, designing everything in detail, from playground to furniture, with just the right touch of animation and fantasy.

Rios's work in the area of garden design has been described as an art form. He has a knack for turning a mundane backyard into a mood-filled landscape, where vegetation, flowers, fountains, and pools coalesce to bring a sense of peace and serenity.

135

Serving as a contrast to the surrounding indigenous landscape of Griffith Park, in Los Angeles, this garden design enhances a house built in the 1950s. Previously an unattractive yard with barbecue pit and minimal vegetation, the rescued area is now enclosed by a dramatic blue mosaic tile that curves around a swimming pool. A fishpond (opposite) extends the floor plan of the glass-walled living room into the garden.

This child care center for MCA/Universal in Los Angeles typifies the effort made by major corporations to provide high-quality environments for their employees' benefit. The boomerang-shaped complex is flooded with natural light.

The Warner Bros. child care center, Burbank, California, is a 9,500-square-foot facility designed with lots of color and animation. Playful facades happily accept the children's designs as well as the corporation's logo.

Perched on a steep rocky outcrop, this house overlooking Storm King Mountain near Garrison, New York, rises above the treetops to take advantage of the dramatic views.

Material moderns

Robert Rogers and Jonathan Marvel, both of whom received architectural degrees from Harvard University, have an enviable record of experience. Rogers worked for I. M. Pei and Partners on projects such as the Louvre in Paris; Marvel worked for Emilio Ambasz, Peter Eisenman, and Richard Meier (on the Getty Museum project in California). They joined forces in 1991 and opened their Tribeca, New York, office with a goal to achieve independence and their own signature on big buildings. Among their major commissions have been the Kunsthalle, a multiple-use facility for arts-related activities, and the renovation of Pratt Institute's School of Architecture, a venerable building dating back to 1868. These projects resulted from the team's successful renovation of El Museo del Barrio, an 8,000-square-foot gallery with exhibition spaces.

While Rogers and Marvel concur that they are modern architects, they are far more interested in construction methods than surface appearance. For example, they don't believe in designing sculptural objects without reference to the surroundings. Their modernistic attitude is more friendly toward the site and undoubtedly gets the respect of their clients.

Born in Colorado, Rogers brings a pioneering spirit to the drafting table, while Marvel, born and brought up in Puerto Rico, has a zestful approach. They enjoy batting ideas back and forth and

They are far more interested in construction techniques than surface appearance

improving on initial concepts. In Cody, Wyoming, three private residences have come to fruition through their combined efforts – all demonstrating that traditional construction and modern materials can make for comfortable, satisfying surroundings.

141

Built for family entertaining, the Hudson Valley house (above) has sweeping rooms and stone terraces, tied together with a curved wall.

The offices for the non-profit Visiting Neighbors organization (left), which cares for the homeless elderly, is a demonstration of how functional elegance can be achieved on a budget. The $6,000 project, with its muslin curtain dividers suspended from a conduit attached with goose-arm lighting, won an *Interiors* magazine design award for its ingenuity.

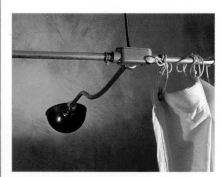

ROBERT ROGERS AND
JONATHAN MARVEL

Located on Buffalo Bill's
original ranch in Cody, Wyoming,
a new residence incorporates one
of the first log structures built on
the property and is set among other
similar vernacular cabins. The
structure is made of sawn lumber
that contrasts with the original
hand-worked logs.

RADICAL

"We must always change, renew, rejuvenate ourselves; otherwise we harden."

Goethe

Although it may be true that the best fruit is often found out on the limb, it requires a determined effort to reach it. But fortunately for the evolution of history, there are always people who are ready to take a risk. Radicals depart from the traditional, the usual, and the expected in their conceptual thinking. Sometimes they take an extreme position. The field of architecture and design is enriched through their innovative minds.

In this century, there have been waves of architects and designers who established new patterns. First came the early turn-of-the-century Arts and Crafts movement. Then the early modernists, with their political ideals of equality and democracy expressed through abstract forms unemcumbered with historic detailing. The mid-century International Style coalesced in the glass curtain wall skyscraper, which crossed cultural barriers to become global architectural iconography. In the 1980s, post-modernism launched a reinvestigation of history, allegory, and meaning, intent on enriching daily experience. By 1990, deconstructionism reflected a world in which political walls came down and multiculturalism dominated.

The radical position evident in this group is focused on forward-looking technology and materials that define the twenty-first century.

The owners of a traditional early twentieth-century stone house designed in the Arts and Crafts tradition in Cincinnati, Ohio, returned from several years in Japan and wanted a "place for tea." The transformation begins in the garden (left) with a sweeping arc of circular wooden stepping stones. The terrace (right) is embellished with symbolic forms in metal and glass, creating a dramatic canopy of visual experience that leads into a serene interior.

From the inside out

Raised in Iowa, schooled at Iowa State and Washington Universities, Terry Brown went on to New York and learned about the Eastern architectural establishment early in his career. He worked for Robert A. M. Stern and Venturi, Scott Brown & Associates. Having investigated formalist doctrines, he then returned to the Midwest and his personal passion: organic architecture. For his inspiration he turned to Midwestern organic architects such as Frank Lloyd Wright and Bruce Goff, with a glance overseas to Antoni Gaudi, Hans Scharoun, and Alvar Aalto.

Brown's work, which has earned him international recognition in Germany, Japan, and Great Britain as well as notice in American publications, is animated, eclectic, and always surprising. Organic architecture is a process of building from the inside out, with the program determining the overall form. The external appearance of the building is a natural result of this process – completely the opposite of the way most architects go about designing a structure. Brown is more concerned with what it is like to walk through a building than whether it is photogenic on the outside. Experiencing the space and the sensation of the atmosphere within is what counts to him. He leans on intuitive thinking rather than mathematical geometry when he designs, a process that leads to remarkably individual, uplifting results.

Concern with what it is like to walk through a building rather than whether it is photogenic on the outside

147

A mosaic of light, introduced
by means of intricate stained-glass
insertions and artworks, occurs
throughout the Tea House.

The architect's own studio has evolved through three schemes to this mushroom-shaped structure, shown here under construction. The unequivocally organic design bridges fantasy and reality.

TERRY BROWN

The Contemporary Arts Center
Bookstore and Artware shop
in downtown Cincinnati, Ohio, is
a museum shop built in an interior
commercial passway. The ornate
decoration recalls the work of
Antoni Gaudi and the artists and
architects of the Art Nouveau period.
Curved and pinwheeled patterns
encrust every surface. Plastic
laminates, marbles, and other
inexpensive materials – even
fossilized rocks – are utilized to
create extraordinary effects.

GISUE HARIRI
AND MOJGAN HARIRI

Redefining modernism

They manipulate tough materials such as steel, bar grating, and wire mesh in ways that paradoxically elicit a romantic quality

Gisue Hariri and Mojgan Hariri are Iranian-born sisters, two years apart in age. They began their architectural collaboration very early on, while still students at Cornell University working on their Bachelor of Architecture degrees. Mojgan went on to pursue academic study in urban design and obtained her Master of Architecture degree at Cornell in 1983. Gisue has devoted time to teaching at various institutions, including Columbia, Yale, Cornell, and McGill Universities and Parsons School of Design.

In 1986 they set up their office together in New York City and immediately began to receive attention for their pristine, inventive ideas. "No young New York firm signals the dawn of the new architectural day more emphatically than Hariri & Hariri," wrote the architecture critic Charles Gandee. Perhaps most notable about their work is the way they manipulate tough materials such as steel, bar grating, and wire mesh in ways that paradoxically elicit a romantic quality. They are particularly adept at this strategy in their furniture designs, having created a beautiful line of lighting fixtures, seating, and a four-poster bed, among other objects.

In 1990 Hariri and Hariri were winners of the Young Architects Forum sponsored by the Architectural League of New York. Their work was also selected among internationally submitted portfolios for the 1990 Young Architects issue of *Progressive Architecture.* They have clients all over the world, bringing their refreshing, pared-down modern idiom wherever they go.

153

An addition and renovation to an existing traditional carriage house built around 1900 in New Canaan, Connecticut, borrows from the familiar forms in the rural New England region, such as barns and covered bridges, but presents them in a dramatic new context.

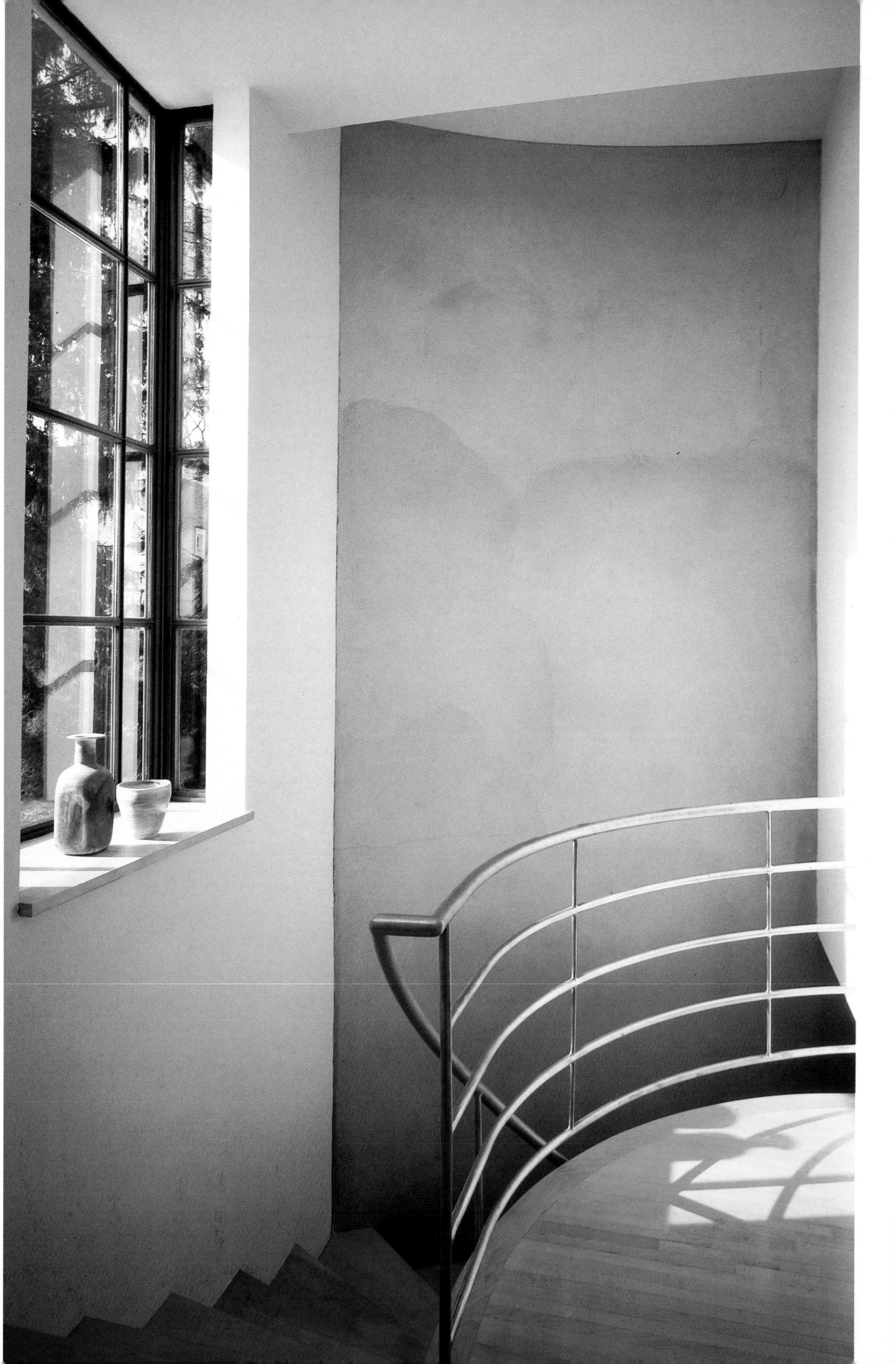

GISUE HARIRI
AND MOJGAN HARIRI

A stucco curvilinear connector
(left, opposite, above) penetrates the
vaulted barn structure, its graceful
stairway and steel railing giving a
presence of today. A new glass-doored
entry (top left) makes a clear
statement.

Pared down to the minimum, the rooms in the house are subordinate to the light and views outside. Steel and wood are used throughout. Kitchen countertops (opposite, below) are steel, as is the bathroom washbasin (left), set into a marble surround with walls and floor of white mosaic tile. The child's room features a play loft (opposite, top).

GISUE HARIRI
AND MOJGAN HARIRI

JSM Music Studios occupies 10,000 square feet on two floors of a Manhattan building in the Flatiron District. A new entry, reception area, waiting room, and administrative offices; a large central lounge for meetings and concerts; support spaces, bathrooms, furniture, and lighting were required to upgrade the environment. Cool colors and materials lend the appropriate rhythms.

159

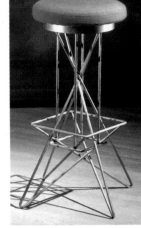

Curvilinear planes come together in a dynamic space where music is the message. A system of melodic design concepts molds the space into an instrument for people who move to a different beat. Furniture is keyed into the same theme.

163

Quality materials transform a small penthouse in Manhattan into a gemlike vision of beauty. Hammered steel forms a mantelpiece that embraces logs for the fireplace in its comfortable curve. Bathroom floor and tub are made of natural cleft slate, with walls of flamed granite and a sink of spun stainless steel. The medicine cabinet is eye-shaped, crowning the overall composition.

The expandable geodesic dome (right) projects to a diameter of eighteen feet, maintaining its shape and stability in all positions. The dome sits on five roller supports. If pulled outward at these points, it expands; if pushed inward, it contracts.

An expanding sphere (opposite) at the Liberty Science Center transforms from a four-and-a-half-foot cluster to an eighteen-foot geodesic sphere. Suspended in the atrium of the New Jersey museum, it continuously opens and closes under motorized control every five seconds.

Fluidity and stability

He has come up with a whole new class of structures that fold and unfold

With a background in both art (Cooper Union) and engineering (Columbia University), Chuck Hoberman sees his goal as inventing new structures and objects using new technologies. He has been so successful in this objective that a thirty-minute documentary was made on his work by the Smithsonian Institution and shown on the Discovery Channel. He already holds five U.S. patents for his expandable structures and has been recognized by NASA for his technical innovations.

When conducting courses on structures at Columbia University's School of Architecture, Hoberman focuses on the need for invention. He teaches that a dialectic exists between discovery and creativity. Discovery is the finding of something that already exists, he says, while creativity is the generation of something that would not otherwise exist. Invention involves both these processes, beginning, he says, "on the fantasy end and ending up on the reality end." His own achievements are proof that this maxim works well. He has come up with a whole new class of structures with developable surfaces that fold and unfold. Along the way, he has demonstrated that this invention can be applied to something as gigantic as a deployable stadium roof that opens and closes according to the seasons, or as small as a briefcase that expands with the job or the papers.

Hoberman uses R. Buckminster Fuller's principle of maximum performance with minimum materials, but he takes Bucky's ideas of geodesic domes to a new frontier. By integrating concepts of fluidity and stability, this structural innovation offers a symbol of the elegant promise of technology.

165

Economy, simplicity, color

When a space is reduced to its bare essentials, it is possible to obtain maximum transformability

Born in Costa Rica, Carlos Jimenez studied architecture at the University of Houston, where he graduated in 1982 with a bachelor's degree and the Best Thesis Design Award. Although he has remained in this Texas city ever since, his work, writings, exhibitions, and academic contributions have taken him all over the world, including Moscow, Madrid, Honolulu, and Helsinki. As a young architect, he has been recognized by the Architectural League of New York, *Progressive Architecture, Architectural Record,* and other publications.

Much of Jimenez's ground-breaking work has been executed in what he describes as residual or marginal pieces of urban space and on stringent budgets. With compactness and simplicity, economical construction and high-energy efficiency, he aims to set standards and introduce a possible reference for the future. He has used his own residence and work spaces as a laboratory to experiment with his ideas. Three individual buildings make up his private working compound; they are linked by a peripheral wooden fence and steel gate, defining a series of garden courtyards. The simple cement-block containers with colorful stucco finished walls have been added to, transformed, and changed during the course of the past decade without drastic alterations. Jimenez believes that when a space is reduced to its bare essentials, it is possible to obtain maximum transformability.

The Jimenez studio in downtown Houston consists of a cluster of simple structures that has evolved and expanded in the course of ten years.

167

Jimenez's house, located across the street from his studio, has an abrupt two-story wall facing north (below top). The large window infuses both interior levels with an ample and gentle quality of light. The ground floor contains two bedrooms, and the upper floor (opposite and bottom) is a loftlike space where only the kitchen and a stairway bookshelf unit divide the open layout. The four container walls of standard masonry block finished with a layered stucco provide the neighborhood of deteriorating one-story wooden houses with a vision of stability.

The Chadwick house is a three-story structure with wood frame and siding in Houston Heights, oriented toward the prevailing southern breezes. Organized on three levels, this 1,600-foot residence is divided into two sections offering contrasting qualities of light and views. A double-height living room (opposite) faces north, overlooking the garden. The south-oriented rooms comprise study, kitchen, and dining and main bedroom, with a vista of the downtown Houston skyline.

The Neuhaus residence occupies the entirety of its double site in Houston by integrating a front and a back courtyard garden into its design (opposite). Constructed of concrete block and stucco exterior walls, with galvanized-steel roofing panels, slate and stained concrete floors, the capacious 5,500-square-foot house is organized in an L-shaped plan. The interior walls are white, creating a neutral backdrop for the owner's collection of antique furniture and contemporary art.

173

High-tech frontiers

Investigations of alternative power sources that encompass building, furniture, and product design

For over twenty years, since the first oil crisis in the 1970s, environmentally conscious architects have been exploring alternative technologies for heating and cooling that make use of renewable energy such as wind, water, and solar power. Since he graduated from Columbia University with a Master of Architecture degree, Canadian-born Gregory Kiss has been investigating new systems and incorporating them into his projects, ranging from private residences to corporate buildings and product designs.

Some of Kiss's buildings have been the first of their kind. For example, he designed the Chronar Corporation's facility for a newly commercialized photovoltaic manufacturing line, with a skylit circulation space shaded by an array of photovoltaic panels that also provide power to the building. As part of an aggressive solar electric program, the New York Power Authority commissioned Kiss to design a demonstration photovoltaic sunshade structure for the Sid Jacobson Jewish Community Center on Long Island. The canopy, constructed of welded steel trees woven with photovoltaic units topped with mesh panels, powers a nearby foundation and a series of rotating fans. The trees are envisioned as modular units that can be assembled in any number of groupings and serve as power providers.

Kiss's investigation of alternative power sources has also encompassed furniture and product design. His bird's-eye maple boardroom table, large enough to seat twenty-two people, is inlaid with photovoltaic panels. The ambient light is sufficient to generate enough power for a low-wattage lighting device at the center of the table. Kiss also developed a solar-power portable lantern for use on camping trips or in areas without electricity.

175

The 7,000-square-foot Chronar Corporation facility was designed to accommodate newly commercialized photovoltaic production technologies. A tile-pattterned two-story block accommodates employee services, while the electrical, chemical, and mechanical facilities are hidden behind a white screen wall. An array of photovoltaic panels shades the skylit circulation area.

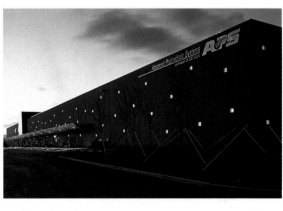

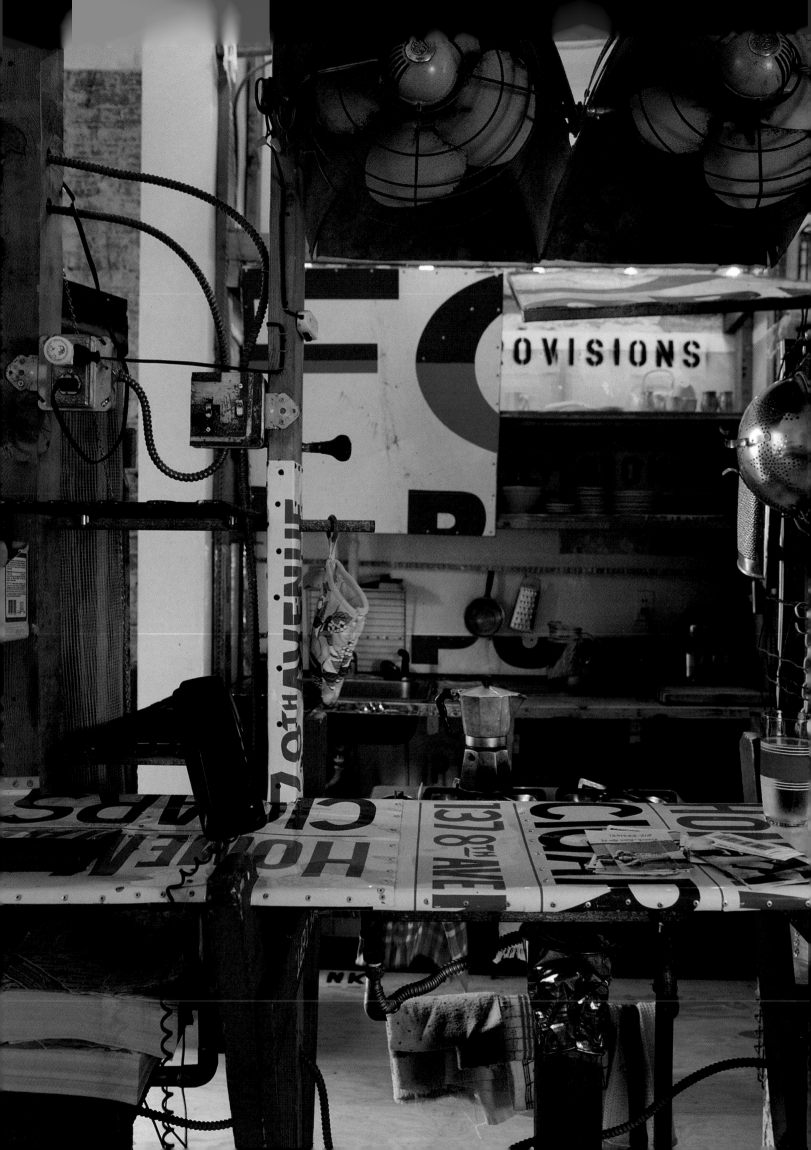

Responding to environmental concerns

Ada Tolla and Giuseppe Lignano were both born in Naples, Italy, within months of each other, grew up in the same district, went to the same primary school, and entered Naples University of Architecture, where they began to collaborate around the time of their graduation in 1989. They subsequently traveled together in the United States and received scholarships in post-graduate architectural studies at Columbia University.

Influenced by the urban scene in New York City, they set up a studio in the West Village and proceeded to win friends and clients with their furniture and interior design elements made from waste materials. By foraging the streets, disassembling and reassembling, they have brought the concept of recycling to an artistic form that stirs the conscience of urbanites concerned about garbage. Lignano and Tolla have created a new aesthetic by confronting the chaos endemic in the contemporary urban life. New York store owners and young, hip apartment dwellers intent on being politically correct seek out Lignano and Tolla to redo their spaces. The results startle the eye and stimulate conversation.

By foraging the streets, disassembling and reassembling, they have brought the concept of recyling to an artistic form

In a conventional floor-through apartment in a Chelsea, Manhattan, brownstone, the kitchen walls have been removed to access the dining/living room. The cooking area is now an assemblage of found and recycled objects and bared appliances, and includes two police barricades that support a metal sign acting as the counters (opposite). Due to limited space, the answering machine has been buried into the surface. Taken out of its housing, the oven hangs from the ceiling (above). Milk crates provide storage containers. Over the sink, pulleys and magnets activate the square metal sheet doors of the cabinet.

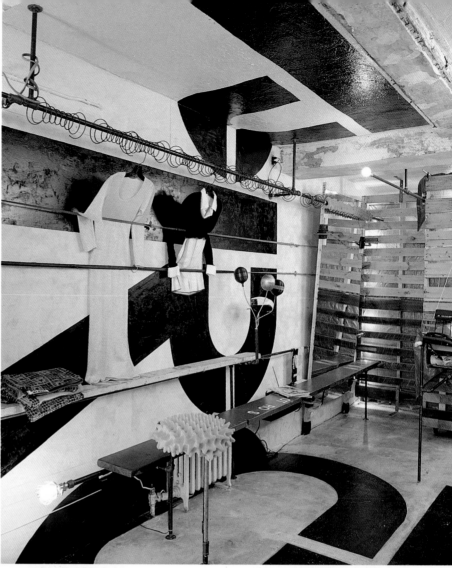

In this Greenwich Village clothing store, the graphic of the store sign is folded into a three-dimensional conformation (floor, side walls, and ceiling) juxtaposed against the square element of the back wall, which is hung with lumber recycled from shipping pallets. Blue tarpaulin rolls down from the back wall to generate a fitting room.

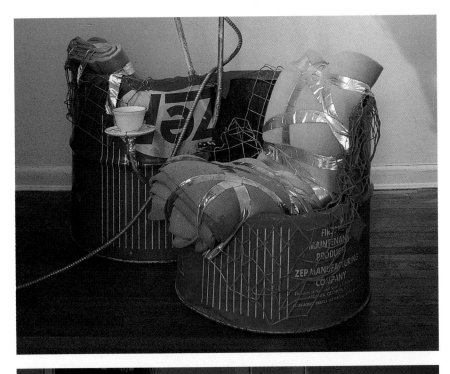

Random encounters with urban refuse result in the construction of real-use furnishings. The electronic workstation (bottom left) evolved out of such diverse items as a broom pole, an antiquated fan, electrical tape, a painting tray, and sundry pieces of wood and metal. The table lamp (above) is made from a recycled plastic detergent container. Two recycled oil drums upholstered with found foam make the tête-à-tête sofa (top left).

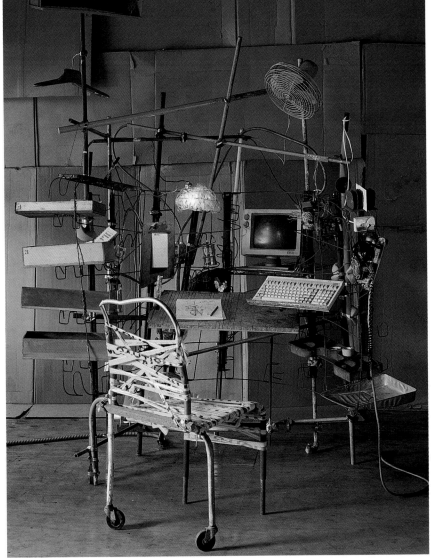

The movable video room (below) with styrofoam mattress offers a new option for couch potatoes. The structure is made from 400 discarded videotape cassettes held within a wooden framework.

Opening up closet space in a restricted apartment, a new facade of shipping-crate wood leads into a clothes storage area on one side and a boudoir makeup space on the other (left).

Multiple detergent bottles make a
colorful floor lamp (above).

Two doors were put to
new use in the foyer of an Upper
West Side Manhattan apartment (top
and left) to make a "hang-it-all"
component for hats, coats,
umbrellas, telephone and message
center, and even bicycle storage.

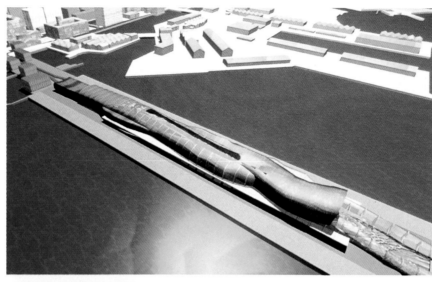

A proposal for a design competition for a Japanese cruise ship terminal is composed of two interlocking structures, one made of tensile fabric and one of metal. The structure and interiors of these unconventional buildings are intended to match the expectations of leisure-seeking Japanese who want to step into a world of almost science fiction fantasy when going on vacation.

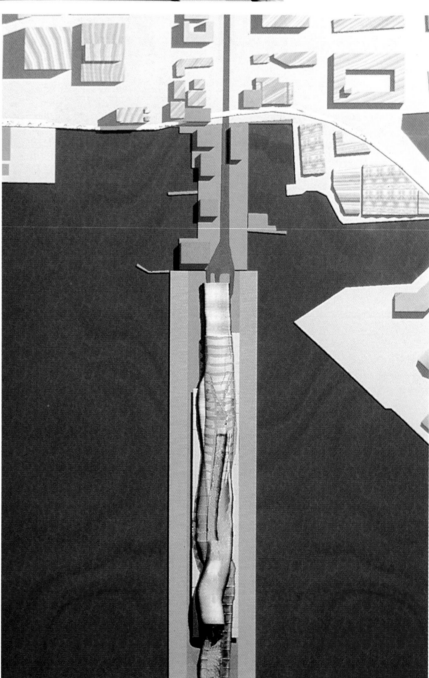

Edge of the future

Sculptural, free-flowing forms express architecture in a way that no one else sees possible

Greg Lynn's academic accolades disclose an unusual combination: architecture and philosophy. He topped off a Bachelor of Philosophy and a Bachelor of Environmental Design from Miami University of Ohio with a Master of Architecture from Princeton. After working in the offices of two star architects, Peter Eisenman and Antoine Predock, he opened his own office in Hoboken, New Jersey.

Lynn's activities are many. He has taught throughout the United States and Europe and is a frequent participant at theoretical conferences all over the world. A member of the board of *ANY*

magazine, the cutting-edge architectural publication, he is a prolific writer of articles explaining the latest theoretical positions in the field. In addition, he is frequently invited to be a juror at academic institutions. As for his practice, his dedicated, ongoing search for unusual form has made him sought after by organizers of major international competitions. His proposed sculptural, free-flowing forms always merit publication (if not construction) because they express architecture in a way that no one else sees possible. Lynn is convinced that future computer technology will realize his ideals.

183

The art of fantasy

*Dense and relentless, his compounded
fragments and fantasies are held together
with comic book memories and a
stroll in a cartoon*

Jordan Mozer has been described as a poet, an artist, and a maker of magic. He is an architect who dreams up fantasies and turns them into hyperactive environments. After graduating with a degree in architecture from the University of Chicago, he set up a studio in an abandoned firehouse and started reaching for the moon. The owners of such restaurants as The Tempest, Americas, Varoom, and

Stars have liked his far-fetched themes and his sympathetic consideration of their goals toward profitability. Mozer's recipe for this financial success lies, he believes, in his attempt to create portraits of his clients. His works are dense and relentless, compounded fragments and fantasies held together with comic book memories, a stroll in a cartoon, with maybe a phrase from Shakespeare thrown in.

No matter what the project or theme, Mozer's

studio always delivers a custom job in which every floor tile, doorknob, wall hook, light fixture, chair, wine cabinet, mirror, mural, stair rail, every rest room sign, is individually handcrafted. To accomplish this feat, Mozer supervises a team of multitalented people who build out and manufacture his one-off ideas. At Iridium, opposite Lincoln Center in New York City, the theme of music and dance inspired door frames in the form of swagged drapes, animated chairs and barstools with feet that suggest leg warmers and toe shoes, pirouetting bronze and blown-glass table lamps wearing tutus, and architectural columns that seem to be wearing tails like orchestra conductors. Even the waiter stations appear to be doing ballet pliés. The hardware for handrails derives from clarinets, and mosaic-tile murals depict crystallized Persian carpets with musical footprint patterns. With such show-stopping charisma, it's no wonder Mozer has won so many design awards.

Iridium, a Manhattan restaurant with a cultural theme, transposes music, ballet, and opera to furniture, flooring, and lighting. Even the lighting fixtures (above) appear to be dancing on their toes.

185

At Iridium, the Placido
Domingo column (opposite)
celebrates the famous tenor in his
tails. Mohair upholstered stools at
Iridium's bar have cast-aluminum
frames that meet the floor like
pointed ballet toe shoes (left). The
maple cabinet (below) has feet in
the ballet dancer's "second position,"
with a pirouetting ballet
lamp on top.

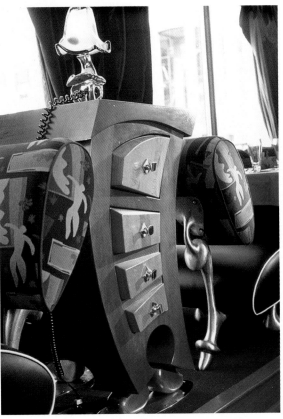

The slumped glass pop art chandelier
(top) at Iridium and the "dripping"
blown-glass light fixture (center) are
meant to represent the fluidity of
music. Orange bellbottom chairs
(bottom) wear platform shoes.

In a typical suburban landscape outside Tokyo, this house was built on a pedestal made by a retaining wall, with a view of a forest and small creek to one side. Concrete block was chosen as the building material for its texture and relationship to the site.

TAEG NISHIMOTO

Abstract to concrete

Precision is the underlying force that makes a design evolve from idea to reality

189

Born and brought up in Japan, Taeg Nishimoto went to Waseda University College of Architecture in Tokyo, where he gained a bachelor's degree, and then crossed the Pacific to study at Cornell University, where he graduated with a Master of Architecture. He has remained in this country ever since, working as adjunct associate professor at both Pratt Institute and Columbia University and running his office in Brooklyn, New York.

Nishimoto's award-winning, cutting-edge designs come from analyzing the geometry of the site, the program, and the specific set of "materialities." He begins with the abstract idea, then focuses on the chronological aspects of the project — what happened, what is happening, and what will happen. Whether simple or complex, those issues interact with other associations and phenomena to generate the final composition. As a young, emerging architect, Nishimoto believes he is in the right place at the right time. After a period of theoretical investigation and metaphorical discourse that has been prevalent in the profession, he sees a renewed excitement in the realities of building, leading to concrete results.

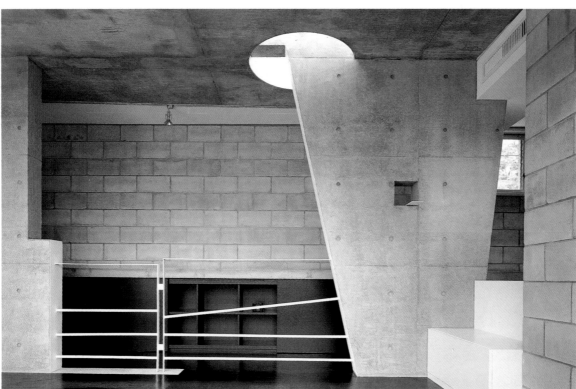

In the interior of the Tokyo house, concrete walls are partially painted and the cork flooring is in two different colors. Angled lines articulate the design of the doors and other details.

Partially embedded into the
ground, this house in Lahaska,
Pennsylvania (shown in model
form), has a steel-frame structure
that lifts the bedrooms up in
the air to take advantage of a
mountain-side view overlooking
a small pond and brook.

The program Super Piers
called for images of a new structure
that would transform the site, an
urban waterfront with derelict piers.
This proposal (shown in model
form left and below) uses
outdoor sports courts as
the connecting element of the
whole building. The ground level
is for tennis, basketball, and
volleyball, the upper level for café,
gym, and other facilities.

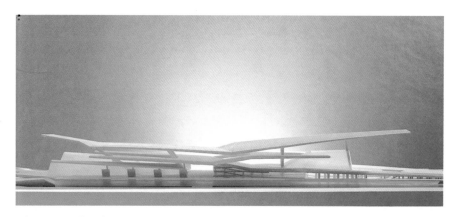

A shipping terminal in Tokyo
presents an image of high-tech grace
and serenity.

The Steel Cloud (below),
the winning entry to the West Coast
Gateway competition, is meant to
communicate the invisible trajectories
of speed and technology in the
twenty-first century.

HANI RASHID
AND LISE ANNE COUTURE

Brave new world

Exploring theory and practice in a multicultural society

Hani Rashid and Lise Anne Couture embody the concept of globalism in contemporary society. Rashid was born in Egypt, brought up in England and Canada, and received his Master of Architecture degree from Cranbrook Academy. Although Couture was born and raised in America and received a Master of Architecture degree from Yale, she partners with him in projects all over the world. Their firm, Asymptote, was established in New York in 1988 and has received recognition for numerous urban competition projects in Italy, Egypt, Moscow, Germany, Holland, France, and Japan.

While most of their projects have yet to be built, Rashid and Couture reside in the front rank of modern architectural discourse because they push the envelope of design, no matter what the program. Their Steel Cloud, the winning entry for the West Coast Gateway competition held by the City of Los Angeles, is a 1,600-foot-long linear structure suspended over the Hollywood Freeway. It was conceived as an assemblage of museums, cinemas, a theater, a park, and aquariums to attract visitors – a counterpart to the Statue of Liberty in New York. Rashid and Couture believe radical ideas can be transformed into built architecture that functions successfully. Hence the name of their firm: in mathematics, the term *asymptote* describes two lines that never actually meet. Rashid and Couture see these two lines as a metaphor for theory and practice in architecture, but have determined that they will focus on both, attempting to "occupy the space between."

195

The Tohoku Historical Museum in northern Japan celebrates the agrarian culture and heritage of the region. Its glass-enclosed halls extend out into canals and rice fields.

Building on memory

He dislikes spaces that are directed by architecture, preferring a more fluid resolution that develops from the nature of the building

Rebelling against the sameness of storefront windows, this high-fashion clothing store has a convex glass facade and monumental plywood sculptures that represent enlarged fragments of the human torso.

Born in Tehran, brought up in London, and educated at university level in Italy, where he received degrees in architecture and urban planning, Michele Saee moved to the United States in 1983. After working for two years in the studio of Morphosis in Los Angeles, he opened his own atelier and has

produced some of the most cutting-edge design on the West Coast. News of his creativity has spread far and wide and he has been featured in numerous publications in the U.S., Japan, England, and Italy.

Saee has put his special touch on restaurants, clothing stores, residences, and even a cosmetic dental clinic, which transformed the notion of what a dental

office should be. Saee's point of view runs counter to that of many other designers. He dislikes spaces that are directed by architecture, preferring a more fluid resolution that develops from the nature of the building. He capitalizes on existing conditions, enhancing them for the project at hand. In this manner, he builds memory, which he believes is a crucial component in whatever a designer produces. "Memory is what makes our lives. Life without memory is no life at

all...our memory is our coherence, our reason, our feeling," he states, quoting the Spanish filmmaker Luis Bunuel. "Without it we are nothing."

Walking through Saee's interiors is like walking through sculpture. He bends ceilings, curves walls, sculpts forms and surfaces which heighten the senses. By so doing, he attempts to resonate with the deeper meaning of design and to reflect the social and human values of the times.

197

Curvilinear shapes
throughout the clothing
store refer to the human
physique. A second level
of inspiration for the shop,
which is located near
Venice, California, came
from boat construction,
an influence that is
explored in the forms
and the wood finishes
of the interiors.

A Los Angeles dental clinic employs light and color to generate serenity and calm, embracing patients in an atmosphere of modern elegance.

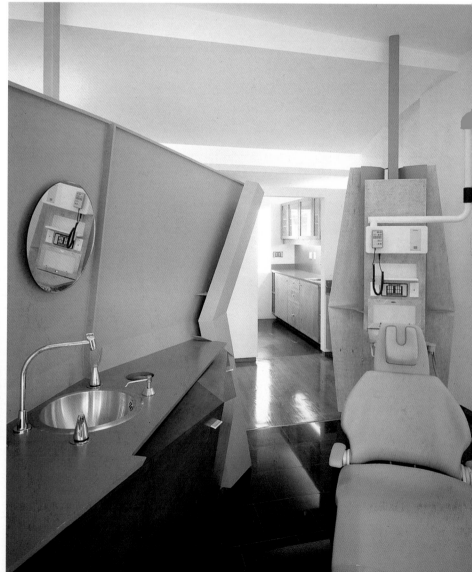

The interior and the exterior of a Los Angeles residence manipulate light and shadow for maximum effect.

The Angeli del Mare restaurant, located in an uninspiring shopping mall at Marina del Rey, California, is treated with a trellislike ceiling constructed of wooden louvers. The greenish stained wood floor, the overscale decorative water lily forms made out of wood, and other fishlike motifs evoke an aquatic feeling entirely appropriate for a seafood restaurant.

Lodge poles and tripod-lashed connections make bold construction elements in this timbered cottage at Dorland Mountain Arts Colony. A solar heating system, along with screens and shutters instead of glass surfaces, bring the owners close to nature.

Provocative matters

He is just as comfortable using wood construction systems as concrete, glass, and steel

Born in Ann Arbor, Michigan, Clark Stevens has gone from coast to coast in his education and practice of architecture. He gained his undergraduate architectural degree at the University of Michigan and then went on to get a master's degree at Harvard. After spending two years in the Chicago offices of Skidmore, Owings & Merrill, Stevens moved to the West Coast, where the architectural scene responds more positively to his leading-edge ideas.

He first joined the offices of Morphosis, known for its radical, modern style using hard-edge materials. While there he collaborated on the design of lighting that is now distributed on the marketplace, as well as the prize-winning entry for the Berlin Library. In 1991 he left with one of the partners, Michael Rotondi, to form a new firm called Roto Architects, which tackles a wide variety of building types, from large-scale commercial to residential and cultural.

While the aesthetics of contemporary West Coast building are likely to encompass concrete, glass, and steel, Stevens is by no means limited to this high-tech vocabulary. He is just as comfortable using wood construction systems, or whatever local materials come to hand on the site, and interfacing with natural systems, such as sun and wind, for heating and cooling. With these principles, he managed miraculously to build a cottage at the Dorland Mountain Arts Colony for $30,000.

205

Divided into three zones – one for children that includes a pool, another for living, and a third for adult sleeping quarters – this Los Angeles house (under construction in these photographs) creates order out of an apparent disorder in its unexpected juxtapositions of forms and materials.

Using light, color, window
frames, and a field of mirrors
to trace movement, daylight, and
people, this conceptual installation
generates insights into how people
view architecture and the views
within and without architecture.
Birch plywood and solid
birch stock put together with oak
dowels express craftsmanship
in a side chair intended for
mass production (opposite).

Art in construction

Seeking the extraordinary in the mundane to gain new insights

Mark Wamble's educational background – Texas A & M for an environmental design degree, Cambridge University, England, and the Harvard Graduate School of Design for a Master of Architecture – seems conventional beside the work he has accomplished. As a project architect for Peter Eisenman between 1983 and 1991, he was involved with several award-winning competition projects, including the Columbus Convention Center, the Rebstockpark Urban Design in Frankfurt, Germany, the Carnegie Mellon Research Center, and the Wexner Center for the Visual Arts, as well as textiles for Knoll. He was also on the winning competition team for the Steel Cloud in Los Angeles (see Rashid and Couture).

Wamble has always integrated practice with teaching, and since 1991 has been an assistant professor at the School of Architecture, Rice University, Houston, while running his own firm, Interloop Architecture and Design. His parallel interest in artistic endeavor is reflected in his responsibilites as Director of the Farish Gallery and Gallerywork at Rice. Wamble's mental agility allows for a broad range of projects, from real-world building to conceptual art exhibitions and furniture designs, all of which strive to change perceptions of the norm.

Aerodynamics for the next century

He strives to get away from buildings that are static, believing that movement and complexity are an expression of our times

On Golden Beach, Florida, this residence occupies the foundations of a 1930s house, but its dynamic character is unmistakably 1990s. It consists of two wings that merge at the entry, family room, and living areas. The front facade facing the street (shown here) is solid masonry, broken by a magnificent onyx, stainless steel, and glass wall that filters afternoon light throughout the house.

Carlos Zapata was born in Venezuela and grew up in Ecuador. He now lives and works in Miami, where the Latino rhythms synchronize with his South American roots. For his architectural training he attended Pratt Institute and Columbia University, and upon graduation with a master's degree, he decided to remain in New York City. It was while working for major architectural firms in Manhattan that his talent was first noted. After a year in Eli Attia's office, he joined Ellerbe Becket, where he stayed for five years, rising to design director and vice president, and winning a roster of awards for the firm.

Zapata's buildings have the feeling of belonging to the twenty-first century. They are exuberant, exciting, and seem to connect with the Space Age in their soaring, floating steel planes and aerodynamic qualities. He strives to get away from buildings that are static, believing that movement and complexity are an expression of our own times and lives. But it is not only on the exterior that this futuristic artistry is expressed. Zapata's attention to the interiors is focused down to the finest detail of hardware or the leg of a piece of furniture.

While he has been involved in many mega-projects, such as the multi-billion-dollar redesign of JFK Airport, multiuse complexes with condominiums and retail space, major office buildings, and hotels, Zapata is a designer who likes to change from scale to scale. Even in a modest 1,800-square-foot two-bedroom apartment he will bring his creative powers to bear, producing unique ideas for decoration and furniture with his own unmistakable cutting-edge signature.

209

Large spans of glass
are used at the back of the
house to open up the interior
spaces to uninterrupted
views of the Atlantic Ocean.
The free-flowing spaces and
modern furniture of this
6,000-square-foot residence
match the aerodynamic
detailing throughout the
house, which includes
steel cables for stairways
and steel riveted paneling
for doors.

The 600-square-foot, bilevel guest house and studio, situated next to the pool and beach, serve as a design studio and open up entirely to the seaview. A motorized panel lifts and descends across the exterior facade to shade the interior from the eastern sun.

The headquarters for a Latin American investment group, the offices of JPBT Advisors, Inc., is on Brickell Avenue in the heart of Miami's business district. The 8,000-square-foot space is orchestrated in cherry wood, stainless steel, glass, blue macauba stone from Brazil, and libra stone from Spain, all manipulated into a very modern image. The corporate "open door" determined the layering of glass partitions to connect views of Biscayne Bay outside for everyone working in the space.

THE FORTY UNDER FORTY

KIMBERLY ACKERT
Ackert Architecture
400 East 55th Street, 15F
New York, NY 10022
212.832.3603

STAN ALLEN
Stan Allen Architect
274 Water Street
New York, NY 10038
212.226.2161

JAY BAKER
Jay Baker Architects
2627 Kipling
Houston, TX 77098
713.520.5446

MOJDEH BARATLOO
CLIFTON BALCH
Baratloo-Balch Architects
155 West 88th Street
New York, NY 10024
212.873.6450

KAREN BAUSMAN
67 East 11th Street,
Suite 617
New York, NY 10003
212.473.3077

DAVID M. BIAGI
2801 Shelbyville Road
Shelbyville, KY 40065
502.633.2885

MARLON BLACKWELL
359 N. Washington Avenue
Fayetteville, AR 72701
501.582.5634

TERRY BROWN
Terry Brown Architect
3331 Erie Avenue
Cincinnati, OH 45208
513.321.1201

VICTORIA CASASCO
Victoria Casasco Studio
320 D. Sunset Avenue
Venice, CA 90291
310.399.1206

JAMES CHILDRESS
Centerbrook Architects
P.O. Box 955
Essex, CT 06426
203.767.0175

KIM COLEMAN
MARK CIGOLLE
Cigolle & Coleman
455 Upper Mesa Road
Santa Monica, CA 90402
310.454.3684

KATHRYN DEAN
CHARLES WOLF
Dean/Wolf Architects
51 White Street
New York, NY 10013
212.219.8714

GILLES DEPARDON
KATHRYN OGAWA
Ogawa/Depardon:
Architecture and
Interior Design
10 Downing Street, #6M
New York, NY 10014
212.627.7390

ROBIN DONALDSON
Shubin + Donaldson
Architects, Inc.
629 State Street, Suite 242
Santa Barbara, CA 93101
805.966.2802

TED FLATO
Lake/Flato Architects,Inc.
311 3rd Street
San Antonio, TX 78205
210.227.3335

LESLIE GILL
63 Greene Street,
Suite 304
New York, NY 10012
212.334.8011

GISUE HARIRI
MOJGAN HARIRI
Hariri & Hariri
18 East 12th Street
New York, NY 10003
212.727.0338

TOM HANRAHAN
VICTORIA MEYERS
445 West 19th Street
New York, NY 10011
212.989.6026

BRIAN HEALY
169 Monsignor O'Brien
Highway, 7th Floor
Cambridge, MA 02141
617.868.6533

JORGE HERNANDEZ
Jorge L. Hernandez Architect
5726 San Vicente Street
Coral Gables, FL 33146
305.666.2181

CHUCK HOBERMAN
Hoberman Associates, Inc.
472 Greenwich Street, #7
New York, NY 10013
212.219.8630

CARLOS JIMENEZ
Carlos Jimenez
Architecture Studio
1116 Willard Street
Houston, TX 77006
713.520.7248

JOHN KEENEN
TERENCE RILEY
Keenen/Riley, NYC
142 West 14th Street, #600
New York, NY 10011
212.645.9210

GREGORY KISS
Kiss & Company
150 Nassau Street
New York, NY 10038
212.513.1713

SULAN KOLATAN
WILLIAM MACDONALD
Kolatan/MacDonald Studio
520 West 14th Street,
Suite 41
New York, NY 10025
212.864.3051

GIUSEPPE LIGNANO
ADA TOLLA
LOT/EK
55 Little West 12th Street
New York, NY 10014
212.255.9326

GREG LYNN
Greg Lynn FORM
161 Tenth Street
Hoboken, NJ 07093
201.798.3665

SCOTT MARBLE
KAREN FAIRBANKS
66 West Broadway, #600
New York, NY 10007
212.233.0653

DAVID T. MAYERNIK
David T. Mayernik Architect
& Painter
25 Monroe Place, #4A
Brooklyn Heights, NY 11201
718.855.0764

JORDAN MOZER
228 West Illinois Street,
2nd Floor
Chicago, IL 60610
312.661.0060

TAEG NISHIMOTO
Taeg Nishimoto +
Allied Architects
253 Washington Avenue
Brooklyn, NY 11205
718.398.1126

WHITNEY POWERS
Studio A, Inc.
12A Vanderhorst Street
Charleston, SC 29403
803.577.9641

THOMAS NORMAN
RAJKOVICH
817 Judson Avenue, I-W
Evanston, IL 60202
708.332.2782

HANI RASHID
LISE ANNE COUTURE
Asymptote Architecture
36 West 15th Street, #3
New York, NY 10011
212.645.3335

MARK RIOS
Rios Associates, Inc.
8008 West 3rd Street
Los Angeles, CA 90048
213.852.6717

ROBERT ROGERS
JONATHAN MARVEL
Rogers Marvel Architects
145 Hudson Street
New York, NY 10013
212.941.6718

MICHELE SAEE
Building
3219 Glendale Boulevard
Los Angeles, CA 90039
213.913.2877

CLARK STEVENS
ROTO Architects, Inc.
600 Moulton, #305
Los Angeles, CA 90031
213.226.1112

MARK WAMBLE
INTERLOOP ARCHITECTS
2480 Times Boulevard, #210
Houston, TX 77005
713.527.9060

CHARLES WARREN
Charles Warren Architect
1239 Broadway
New York, NY 10001
212.689.0907

CARLOS ZAPATA
Carlos Zapata
Design Studio
419 A. Española Way
Miami Beach, FL 33139
305.672.9435

PROJECT CREDITS

KIMBERLY ACKERT
ACKERT ARCHITECTURE
Design partner:
 Kimberly Ackert
Administrative Partner:
 Robert Brown
Team participants:
 Patricia Gosling
 Julia Gordon
Interiors: Caroline Casey

STAN ALLEN
STAN ALLEN ARCHITECT
Avery Hall Computer Design
 Studios
Client: Columbia University
 Graduate School of
 Design
Architect: Stan Allen
Assisted by: Lyn Rice
Additional assistance by:
 Katherine Kim
 Anna Mueller

Bill Arning Loft
Client: Bill Arning
Architect: Stan Allen
Assisted by: Catarina Tsang

JAY BAKER
JAY BAKER ARCHITECTS
Roper Residence
Project designer: Jay Baker
Project team:
 Robert Civitello
 Phil Schowe

Bayshore on the Boulevard
Project designer: Jay Baker
Project team: Bill Briggs
 Cathy Boswell
 Robert Civitello

Brad Crown
Tom Figgins
Dan Hassebrook
Randy Lore
Michael Mallone
Joe Price
Phil Schowe
Syn Thanapura
Russell Zeidner

Light Spikes
Project designer: Jay Baker
Project team: Eva Belik

MOJDEH BARATLOO,
CLIFTON BALCH
BARATLOO-BALCH
ARCHITECTS
Shamana
Lighting design: Johnson
 Schwinghammer
Decorative painting:
 Rebecca Martin
Metal leaf:
 Georgia Matsumoto
Display case fabrication:
 Rohner Furniture

KAREN BAUSMAN
LESLIE GILL
Huxford Residence
Designers: Karen Bausman
 Leslie Gill, partners in
 charge with
 Scott Marble
Architect of record:
 Bruce Aaron Parker
Presentation drawings:
 Paivi Jaaskelainen

Prichett Residence
Design team:
 Karen Bausman,
 Leslie Gill, partners in

charge, Adi Shamir
 associate, Alison Berger
 Paivi Jaaskelainen
 Clarissa Matthews
 Bette Miller
 Tim Schollaert
Model builder: Carl Miller
Presentation drawings:
 Elizabeth Alford
 Alex Porter
 Homa Shojaie

Warner Bros. Records
Design team:
 Karen Bausman, partner
 in charge with
 Alison Berger,
 Adi Shamir
Project architect:
 David Wilbourne
Project team:
 John Blackmon
 Denise DeCoster
 John Ginocchio
 Alicia Imperiale
 Rob Luntz
 Kevin McClurkan
 Ann O'Dell
 Jackie Pilliciotti
 Bryce Sanders
 Gary Shoemaker
 Mabel Wilson
Presentation drawings:
 James Hicks
 Nandini Bagchee

Constellation Screen
Designer: Karen Bausman
Project manager:
 John Ginocchio
Fabricators:
 Gamm Kagan
 Waterjet Industries
 Richard Webber
 Metal Fabricators
Sponsor: Susan Lewin,
 Formica Corporation

Optometry Store
Designers: Karen Bausman
 Leslie Gill
Contractor: All American
Furniture: Bausman Gill
Screen: Karen Bausman
 Leslie Gill
 Scott Marble
Lights: Jerry Style

DAVID M. BIAGI
DAVID M. BIAGI ARCHITECT
Assistant:
 J. Quintin Biagi, Jr.

MARLON BLACKWELL
June Moore Residence,
 Cashiers, North Carolina
Architect: Marlon Blackwell
Project assistants:
 Kent Duckham
 Tim Mulavey
 Charles Rotolo
Contractor: Cashiers Valley
 Construction,
 Cecil Houston
Project manager engineer:
 John Looney (structural)

Audesse Garden House and
 Formal Garden, Wenham,
 Massachusetts:
Architect: Marlon Blackwell
Project assistant:
 Kent Duckham
Landscape architect:
 Jim Heroux
Engineer:
 John Looney (structural)

Flynn-Schmitt Residence,
 Wedington, Arkansas
Architect: Marlon Blackwell
Contractor: Tubb Robinson
Engineer:
 Joe Looney (structural)

TERRY BROWN
TERRY BROWN ARCHITECT
The work we make in my
studio continues to benefit
from the support and
expertise of my associate

Steven Brown and from the enthusiastic labors from the seemingly continuous flow of students of architecture, all young at heart, that pass through.

VICTORIA CASASCO
VICTORIA CASASCO STUDIO
Aznar Residence
Architects: Victoria Casasco
  Carlos Garcia-Delgado
Construction supervision:
  Chomeo-Mestre
Engineer:
  Carlos Garcia-Delgado

Appell Residence
Architect: Victoria Casasco
Assistants: John DuBard
  Julia Cox
  Thomas Lee White
  Martin Mullin
Model: Bill McMullen
Contractor:
  Bowman/Ficarra
  Construction
Engineer:
  Johnson/Creekmore/
  Fabre Consulting
  Engineers

JAMES CHILDRESS
CENTERBROOK
ARCHITECTS
Pond House, New England
Architects:
  James C. Childress, AIA
  and Mark Simon, FAIA
Design team:
  Paul Shainberg, AIA
  Stephen Holmes, AIA
  Kevin Henson, AIA

House in the Connecticut hills, Connecticut
Architects:
  James C. Childress, AIA,
  and Mark Simon, FAIA
Design team:
  Charles G. Mueller, AIA

Erle Residence, Guilford, Connecticut
Architects:
  James C. Childress, AIA,
  and Paul Shainberg, AIA
Design team:
  Christopher Arelt

KATHRYN DEAN
CHARLES WOLF
DEAN/WOLF ARCHITECTS
Peeled Perimeter Library
Project assistant:
  Elizabeth Whittaker
Contractor: Tetsu Usui

Inside Outside Studio
General contractor:
  Seth Melchert

Spiral House
Engineer:
  Anchor Consulting
  Evan Akselrad
Contractor:
  Dowko Development,
  Rich Donsavage
*Site and concrete
  contractor:* Einar Moi

GILLES DEPARDON
KATHRYN OGAWA
OGAWA/DEPARDON
Villino Monteverde
Architects: Kathryn Ogawa
  Gilles Depardon
Structural engineer:
  Hage Engineering
  Marc Hage
Landscape: Paola Chessa
Contractor: Gino Spada
Carpenter: Fratelli Acardo

ROBIN DONALDSON
SHUBIN + DONALDSON
ARCHITECTS
Trout Club Residence
Project architect:
  Robin Donaldson, AIA
Associated architect:
  Russell Shubin, AIA

Project team: Dawn Sherry
  Nancy Chen

Cut-out Chair
Project architect:
  Robin Donaldson
Project team: Jim Bell
  Thomas Hashbarger
  Jaime Morrison

TED FLATO
Lake/Flato Architects

Chandler Ranch
Design team: Ted Flato
  David Lake
  John Grable

Carrarro
Design team: Ted Flato
  David Lake
  Graham Martin

El Tule
Design team: Ted Flato
  David Lake
  Juaquin Escamilla
  Robert Trinidad

Lasater Ranch
Design team: Ted Flato
  David Lake
  Karla Greer

TOM HANRAHAN
VICTORIA MEYERS
Holley residence, New York
Architects: Tom Hanrahan
  Victoria Meyers
Project assistants:
  Martha Coleman
  James Slade
Interior Furnishing:
  Tse-Yun Chu
General contractor:
  J. Lauda Co., Inc.

Custom steel fabrication:
  E. Fabrication
  Scott Enge
Custom cabinetry:
  Europa Woodworking

GISUE HARIRI
MOJGAN HARIRI
HARIRI & HARIRI
New Canaan House
Architects: Hariri & Hariri
Principals in charge:
  Gisue Hariri
  Mojgan Hariri
Design team:
  Andre Bideau
  Yves Habegger
  Kazem Naderi
  Paul Baird
  William Wilson
Structural engineer:
  Ahneman Associates, P.C.
General contractor:
  GOL Construction

JSM Music Studios
Architects: Hariri & Hariri
Principals in charge:
  Gisue Hariri
  Mojgan Hariri
Design team: Paul Baird
  Martha Skinner
  John Bennett
  Harry Zernik
Structural engineer:
  Robert Silman Associates
Contractor: Jogran, Inc.
Metal fabrication:
  Kern/Rockenfield, Inc.
Hologram: Rudy Berkhout

BRIAN HEALY
Projects done in
    collaboration with
    Michael Ryan

JORGE HERNANDEZ
JORGE L. HERNANDEZ
ARCHITECT
Project team: Ana Alvarez
    Francis Lyn
    Omar Morales
    George Pastor
    Roberto Viola-Ochoa

CHUCK HOBERMAN
HOBERMAN ASSOCIATES,
INC.
Metal slides fabrication:
    Bill Record Engineering

CARLOS JIMENEZ
CARLOS JIMENEZ
ARCHITECTURE STUDIO
Jimenez house and studio
Project team:
    Carlos Jimenez, designer
    Dominique Brousseau
    Robert Fowler

Chadwick House
Project team:
    Carlos Jimenez, designer
    Dominique Brousseau
    Eric Batte

Neuhaus House
Project team:
    Carlos Jimenez, designer
    Dominique Brousseau
    Robert Fowler
    Eric Batte

JOHN KEENEN
TERENCE RILEY
KEENEN/RILEY
Project team: Seung Jae Lee
    David Small
    Celeste Umpierre
    Patrick Walker
    Jim Yohe

GREGORY KISS
KISS & COMPANY
APS Photovoltaic
Manufacturing Facility
Fairfield, CA
Principal in charge:
    Gregory Kiss
    Kiss Cathcart
Architects:
    Anders Architects, P.C.
Engineers:
    Ove Arup & Partners

SULAN KOLATAN
WILLIAM MACDONALD
KOLATAN/MACDONALD
STUDIO
M Loft
Design principals:
    A. Sulan Kolatan and
    William J. MacDonald
Design team: J. Moustafulos
Structural consultants:
    Guy Nordenson
    Ove Arup & Partners
Contractors:
    Michael Harrington
    Contracting, Inc.
Metal contractor:
    Alvin and Jennifer Cooke
Glass contractor:
    Alan Glazier Glass, Inc.

S/F Apartment
Design principals:
    A. Sulan Kolatan and
    William J. MacDonald

Design team:
    C. Sharpless, A Riley
Structural consultants:
    Guy Nordenson
    Ove Arup & Partners
Contractors:
    Cinar Construction
    Arcon Construction
General metal and glass:
    Alvin and Jennifer Cooke

GREG LYNN
GREG LYNN FORM
Project team:
    Donald Hearn
    Kim Holden
    Christian Hubert
    Edward Keller
    Gregg Pasquarelli
    Amar Sen
    Robert Vertes
Structural design:
    Craig Schwitters
*Computer rendering and
computer modeling:*
    Straylight Imaging

SCOTT MARBLE
KAREN FAIRBANKS
Silverstein/Olson Residence
Architects: Scott Marble
    Karen Fairbanks
Project team:
    Pete Cornell
    Jay Berman
Contractor:
    Up-Rite Construction
Woodwork: Sub Studio

WHITNEY POWERS
STUDIO A, INC.
Project team: Sheri Horton
    Sarah Hargreaves

HANI RASHID
LISE ANNE COUTURE
ASYMPTOTE
ARCHITECTURE
Los Angeles West Coast
Gateway

Principal architects:
    Hani Rashid
    Lise Anne Couture
Project team: Richard Cress
    Raoul Bustos
    Wissam Jabr
    Eytan Kaufman
    Ursula Kurz
    Michelle Lederer
    Marisable Marratt
    Nuno Mateus
    Ignacio Salas
    Begoñia Fernandez-Shaw
    Mark Wamble
    Christopher Warnick
    Beth Weinstein

Yokohama passenger ship
    terminal
Principal architects:
    Hani Rashid
    Lise Anne Couture
Project team:
    William Deegan
    Kevin Estrada
    Jeffrey Johnson
    Diogo S. Lopes
    Paolo Lopes
    Lynne Miyamoto
    Max Müller
    Ryuichi Sasaki

MARK RIOS
RIOS ASSOCIATES, INC.
Schrader Bohnett Residence
Principal: Mark Rios
*Project architect/project
designer:* Julie Smith

MCA/Universal Child Care
Center
Principal: Mark Rios
Project architect:
    Julie Smith
Project designer:
    Frank Clementi
Job captain:
    Jonathan Black
Landscape architect:
    Polly Furr, Dale Wall
Design team: Guido Porto
    Richard Prantis
    Tom Marble
    Virginia Tyler

Warner Bros. Children's
Center
Principal: Mark Rios
*Project architect/project
designer:* Frank Clementi
Job captain: Richard Levy
Landscape architect:
  Charles Pearson
Design team: Julie Smith
  Hsuan-ying Chou
  Virginia Tyler

ROBERT ROGERS
JONATHAN MARVEL
ROGERS MARVEL
ARCHITECTS
Partners: Robert M. Rogers
  Johathan Jova Marvel
Associate: Bodil Pedersen
Team: Deacon Marvel
  Christian Humann

CLARK STEVENS
ROTO
Project: QWFK house
Architect: ROTO
  Michael Rotondi
  Clark Stevens, partners
Team: Michael Brandes
  (Site Supervisor)
  Brian Reiff
  Danny Maselli
  Craig Scott
Assistants: Rebecca Bearss
  Wendy Borg
  Peggy Bunn
  Francis Gutierrez
  Ralf Hochstrasser
  Lisa Iwamoto
  Richard Kasensarm
  Bader Kassim
  Kenneth Kim
  Tracy Loeffler
  Geoff Lynch
  Raul Moreno
  Yusuke Obuchi
  Stuart Spafford
  Caroline Spigelski
  David Teiger
  Michael Yeo
Structural: Joseph Perazzelli
Mechanical: Mel Bilow &
  Associates

Electric: G & W Electrical
  Engineers
Interior decorator:
  Kay Kollar Design
Contractor: F. J. Korfmann
  Contracting Co.
Civil engineering:
  Gladstone Design

Project: Dorland Mountain
  Arts Colony
Architect: ROTO
  Michael Rotondi
  Clark Stevens, partners
Collaborator:
  Yusuke Obuchi
Team: Jim Bassett
  Scott Francisco
  Angela Hiltz
  Jonathan Winton
Assistants: Jim Kim
  Kenneth Kim
  Tracy Loeffler
  Geoff Lynch
  Brian Reiff
  Caroline Spigelski
  Joy Stingone
  Michael Yeo
Builder: ROTO
Color consultant:
  April Greiman
Fabric roofing:
  Rubb West/Azim Jessani
Structural engineer:
  Joseph Perazzelli
Steel fabrication:
  John McCoy

MARK WAMBLE
INTERLOOP ARCHITECTS
Gallery Works
Project team:
  Merrill Alorich
  Stephanie Bassler
  Eran Montoya
  Peony Quan
  Thaddeus Briner
  Jeff Guga
  Sommer Schauer
  Dana Weeder

Bois d'Arc furniture
Project team:
  Begoña Fernandez-Shaw

CHARLES WARREN
CHARLES WARREN
ARCHITECT
Red House
Project assistant:
  Andrew B. Ballard
Furniture builder:
  Bruce Volz

CARLOS ZAPATA
CARLOS ZAPATA DESIGN
STUDIO
Private residence
Design architect:
  Carlos Zapata Design
  Studio
Associate architect:
  Una Idea
Design team: Carlos Zapata
  John West
  Catalina Landes
Design contribution:
  Eduardo Calma
  Maria Wilthew
  Frank Gonzalez
  Jose Rodriguez
Project coordinator:
  Melissa Koff
Structural engineer:
  Leslie E. Robertson
  Associates
General contractor:
  Cruz R. Rodriguez
  Associates
Landscape architect:
  Raymond Jungles Inc.

JPBT Advisors Headquarters
Design architect:
  Carlos Zapata Design
  Studio
Associate architect:
  Una Idea
Architect of record:
  Altman Architects
Design team: Carlos Zapata
  John West
  Catalina Landes
Design contribution:
  Eduardo Calma
  Maria Wilthew
  Frank Gonzales
  Jose Rodriguez
Project coordinator:
  Melissa Koff
Structural engineer:
  Santiago & Associates
M/E/P engineer:
  Lauredo Engineering
General contractor:
  Skaf Construction

INDEX OF PHOTOGRAPHERS

223